The purpose of this book is twofold: **(1)** to cast a vision for manhood that can be passed from one generation to another, and **(2)** to invite dads and mentors to bring boys and young men on the definitive spiritual journey, a process (not an event) that involves staying connected over an extended period of time in father-son groups. The quest to become a mature man, inside and out, is influenced not only by individual dads doing their part within each family, but also by the involvement of men in a fellowship that brings fathers together with their sons to discuss important life issues. If this camaraderie continues over a period of years, relationships develop and wisdom is shared. The author's journey of raising his son to adulthood in the context of a vibrant father-son fellowship illuminates the voyage for others.

Fathers and sons must connect at the <u>heart level</u> to assure that each of them will reach their potential. What John Kain and his collaborators have done in their helpful book Fathers And Sons Together is provide you with a reference point and some practical tools to strengthen your relationship with your son. John has collected, refined and tested some of the best ideas to inspire you in your fathering adventure. I encourage you to buy a copy of this book and reflect on his advice.

—Ken R Canfield PhD.
Director, Center for the Family, Pepperdine University
Founder, National Center for Fathering

Fathers And Sons Together™ provides questions at the end of each chapter for personal contemplation, parent strategy sessions, or for use in small groups. The appendices describe tested ways to build connectivity that work in today's culture while avoiding "cookie cutter" formats and also encouraging active involvement from fathers and surrogate dads.

Fathers And Sons Together, Exploring Life's Most Important Relationships

Copyright © 2011 by John Kain

All rights reserved. No part of this book may be reproduced or transmitted in any form or by any means, electronic or mechanical, including photocopying and recording, or by any information storage and retrieval system, without permission in writing from the author.

Fathers And Sons Together is a registered trademark of John Kain for publications and teaching materials in the field of Christian Ministries.

www.fathersons.org

All Scripture quotations are taken from THE HOLY BIBLE, NEW INTERNATIONAL VERSION®, NIV® Copyright © 1973, 1978, 1984, 2010 by Biblica, Inc.™ Used by permission. All rights reserved worldwide.

The boldfaced words in Scripture passages indicate the author's emphasis.

Cover Photo obtained from FOTOSEARCH STOCK PHOTOGRAPHY © 2010. Used by permission.
All rights reserved.

LIBRARY OF CONGRESS
CATALOGING-IN-PUBLICATION DATA
Kain, John.
Fathers And Sons Together: Exploring Life's Most Important Relationships / John Kain—1st edition

1. Family & Relationships / Parenting / Fatherhood
2. Christian Life

Printed in the United States of America
2011—First Edition

This book is dedicated to
Michael, Ina, Joe, and Erin

The Next Generation

TABLE OF CONTENTS

Introduction **1**

Chapter 1 **Men Who Can Relate** **7**
    Relationships Define the Real Man 9
    A Journey of Spiritual Growth 10
    Fathers And Sons Together 12
    Hands Outstretched 13

Chapter 2 **The Bond between You and God** **19**
    Knowing and Trusting God 20
    Listening to the Holy Spirit for Direction 22
    My Work, God's Business 23
    A Prayer for Wisdom 27

Chapter 3 **The Brotherhood of Christian Men** **31**
    Purposeful Fellowship 32
    The Schoolyard Bully 32
    Misconceptions about Friendships 35
    Relationship Repairs 38
    Praying Together 39
    Accountability and Purity 40
    The Hill Cries Out 41
    Sharing a Good Thing with Everyone 43

Chapter 4 **Marriage and Family** **49**
    Healthy Marriages Thrive with Servant Leaders 50
    Where Are You Needed Most? 53
    Family Finances 55
    Capitalizing on Contentment 56

Chapter 5 **A Heart for the Next Generation** **61**
    Relationship Time: Quantity AND Quality 62
    Getting a Handle on Discipline 63
    Passing Along a Unique Perspective 66
    Involvement in a Faith Community 67
    Personal Health 68

Chapter 6 **Father Son Camaraderie** **73**
    Don't Embrace the Generation Gap **73**
    Coming Alongside Your Son **75**
    Guidance from Above and Within **76**
    Breaking from the "Drop Off" Culture **77**
    Pizza and a Hike **78**
    Raising Expectations **80**
    And When He Becomes an Adult… **81**
    Breaking Through **82**
    When You're Ready, Son **85**

Chapter 7 **Let's Get Real** **89**
    Nobody's Perfect **90**
    A Difference from Within **91**
    Honesty and Integrity **93**
    Not the Typical Picture of a Real Man **96**
    Serving with Dad **97**
    Kindness **100**
    Perseverance and Hope **101**

Appendix A **Organizing a Father-Son Group** **105**
    Overcoming Obstacles **107**
    Addressing Age Appropriate Issues **107**
    Ceremonies, and a Father's Blessing **109**
    Meeting Format **111**
    Leadership Recruitment and Scheduling of Activities **112**
    Learning to be Inclusive **114**
    From a Woman's Perspective by Jan Kraushaar **116**

Appendix B **Overview of Meeting Topics** **119**

Appendix C **Spiritual Maturity Principles for Men** **129**

Appendix D **Difficult Questions** **133**
    #1: Why Do Good People Suffer? **134**
    #2: How Can We Understand Predestination **136**
    A Small Sign **138**

Acknowledgments **143**

Introduction

Which is more important to God: (1) the things we accomplish on this earth, or (2) how we relate to Him while we are living in it? If we are good men, perhaps even great men, but we don't have an intimate relationship with God, have we succeeded – can we consider ourselves to be **real men**? On the other hand, if we have a sincere love for God but fail to live up to high standards of moral behavior, are we successful in His view?

A father may tell his son "do these things, and you will be a godly man." Humanly speaking, it's true that men need to perform a certain way to achieve success. We therefore look to performance standards in order to measure our progress toward maturity. That makes perfect sense to those of us who manage and evaluate personnel and make decisions regarding who will advance and how they will be compensated. It's tempting to apply the same principle, to set measurable standards, in regard to spiritual things. Hence our focus on standards for living, including the Ten Commandments – there is the code of behavior son, just go out and do it.

For Christians, the problem with this performance based way of thinking and living is that Jesus takes us to a different place when it comes to defining what is important. He tells us that maturity takes shape in relationships—in our relationship with God and our relationships with people. Once we embrace the primacy of these key relationships, we can make them a part of our daily life and share what we learn about them with our sons and daughters. What we do (how we perform) is important, but how we relate to God and other people is more important because our actions should flow from these relationships. The importance of relationship is highlighted in the following response given by Jesus to a question about priorities.

> "Teacher, which is the greatest commandment in the Law?"
> Jesus replied:
> "'**Love the Lord your God
> with all your heart
> and with all your soul
> and with all your mind.**'
> This is the first and greatest commandment.
>
> And the second is like it:
> '**Love your neighbor as yourself.**'"
> — Matthew 22:36-39

It sounds so simple. Love God, love others. The problem is that love is not just "giving and receiving." It's much deeper than that. It is difficult for most of us to put God's agenda and the needs of others in the forefront of our thoughts. Men tend to think in terms of getting things done rather than growing closer to God or to each other. But the answer Jesus gave suggests that we need to focus on relating to God with our heart, soul and mind. We need to be intentional about love, and our enthusiasm needs to be sincere. It doesn't automatically happen, and we can't fake it. By recognizing both God's expectations and our shortcomings, we can grow in our understanding of love and our ability to love sincerely.

The response Jesus gave is surprising because of what He did not say. He did not focus on being disciplined, righteous or responsible. His focus is on shedding our self centered ways in order to develop intimacy with God. And we are to really care for other people, especially those in need, not just with our words but with our actions.

Making these types of relationships a priority involves a number of personal choices, such as paying attention to our health so that we can think clearly (this is part of the "with all your mind" directive included in the verses above). Our renewed efforts to build genuine connections with people around us will also influence the person we become. Although these things take us out of our self, we soon discover that they enable us to *grow into our new self* – the true self that we discover in Christ, along with the Spirit-empowered character that subsequently enables those manly qualities of discipline, righteousness and responsibility to come alive in us.

This book delves into relationship issues in considerable detail because I have stumbled across them at every turn in the search for what it means to grow up. That search has taken place with many godly men whom I have come to know in the context of **F**athers **A**nd **S**ons **T**ogether™ (**FAST**). The young and older men who gathered in **FAST** groups during the past decade to discuss real life issues have not shied away from tough questions and difficult problems. We have endeavored to understand how God wired each of us and what He wants of us and that process of discovery continues as we mature. It's a process that requires men to carefully consider God's priorities, which build upon our relationship with Him and our relationships with people.

We quickly learn, for example, that relationships involve risk. We see that we need to handle relationships wisely. Even the first step—determining whom we might enter into a relationship with—calls for wisdom. Does that person exhibit good judgment or obviously lack good sense? Will our connection with that individual strengthen our commitment to God, or distract us from a close walk with Him? If that person is needy, hurting, and/or moving away from God, can we extend mercy, grace, and charity without being pulled away from our moral convictions? Good judgment is needed because affection can be easily misunderstood as approval or even the desire for intimacy.

Some of us try to protect ourselves from the potential pain of relationships by drawing inward, but this is not an option for godly men. Instead, we must venture forth into relationships, knowing that challenges are likely to occur, aware that we will sometimes get hurt, and intending to love others with God's love. This book has been written to equip men for a significant spiritual journey with those they love now and those they will touch with God's love in the future. If you are a father, then you already have an opportunity to influence future generations. By connecting or reconnecting with God today, your son or daughter will be impacted tomorrow – your sincere love will make a difference. At the end of your life on this earth, nothing else really matters.

Even if you never knew your own father, older men have probably impacted your life (for better or worse). And if you are a young man, fatherhood may be in your future. These pages will enable and challenge you to grow up and get connected with other men who are brave enough to explore their faith together.

Women will gain perspectives on how to encourage the boys and men in their life, while enhancing their own understanding of what it means to become mature, godly women.

I experienced remarkable things during the past decade with a diverse group of dads who wanted to share the meaning of life with their sons, and decided to gather together with that purpose in mind. By meeting once or twice each month and thoughtfully addressing topics important to men, our understanding of the journey of faith grew. The original father-son group spawned the formation of many other such groups at our church and other churches, and along the way we have learned a lot about relationships, including our inner life with God, our friendships, and our connections with our kids' friends. Lesson plans and other resources for starting and leading such groups are available at **www.fathersons.org**.

1
Men Who Can Relate

We moved slowly up the line for about 20 minutes before reaching the stadium entry door, but the delay was no surprise because security checks have become commonplace at major sport venues. After crawling through roadway traffic congestion on the way into the stadium parking area, this was no big deal. My son Michael and I took the opportunity to chat with other fans.

"Do you think that LT will set a rushing record today?"

>"I hope he does – we need the win."
>
>"It's my first time at an NFL game – who's LT?"
>
>"He'd better get it done today – I bet a lot of money on this game."
>
>"I hope they don't run him, because I think Rivers ought to throw more."
>
>"No way – he's past his prime."

Whether you are a fan of LaDainian Tomlinson (LT) or don't know anything about him, the anticipation and energy associated with 50,000 people gathering in one place is enough to make anyone feel a part of something big. Knowing that this great running back was still running strong and due to setting a rushing record, Michael and I expectantly found our way into the stadium to see what would happen.

Big games, political rallies, and performances by famous musicians bring people together, even if we disagree about the value of their accomplishments. Once any particular athlete or politician or performer has become an item for discussion, then they are also part of our way of relating with friends and family members. We can unite around either our appreciation of their giftedness or our criticism of their abilities. Or we can debate those things. Men like to discuss what is going on in the world around us instead of what is going on inside us, and we often do things together that do not require us to open up and talk about "personal stuff."

Of course, relationship times based upon common interests can be a lot of fun and have lasting significance. My son Michael and I shared many high-fives with Charger fans that day, and LT did not disappoint. During 2007 he passed Walter Payton on the all time football rushing touchdown list with his 111th career touchdown against the Kansas City Chiefs. On December 6, 2009, Tomlinson moved into eighth place on the career rushing list, passing both Jim Brown and Marshall Faulk.

Michael and I will always have the memories of going to a few NFL and NBA games (Chargers and Lakers), but those memories are icing on the cake. We have worked hard at staying close through his transition to manhood, and as his dad I have been intentional about our friendship. Although I appreciate that friendships are most often established and enhanced by shared experiences, I have also learned that real men – godly men who stand for much more than themselves – relate to God and relate to other people in ways that go deeper than the activities they share.

Unfortunately many men don't go beyond "doing stuff together" as a way of relating with one another. In addition, our understanding of a good relationship with God is often limited to the image of an enthusiastic fan within a large crowd watching the Heavenly Father perform from a distance (as opposed to the intimate one-on-one bond that can be present between an earthly son and his spiritual dad).

This propensity for superficial relationships is a problem that is easily passed from father to son. I struggled with this tendency as my son Michael was approaching adolescence and our family schedule became attached to the drop-off routines that are typical of our suburban setting. Our suburban lifestyles (out-of-balance work schedules for dads or overcrowded activity schedules for kids) do not encourage fathers to have a strong mentoring role with their sons regarding spiritual matters. This passivity amongst fathers when it comes to doing their part in leading boys into manhood contributes to a weak understanding of faith amongst many boys and men.

Relationships Define the Real Man

I use the term "real man" throughout this book to describe otherwise ordinary men who have **genuine faith** (a realistic view of God), **genuine hope** (a realistic view of the future which extends beyond our life on this earth), **genuine love** (a realistic view of the inherent value in other people), and **genuine humility** (a realistic view of themselves). We are good examples of real men for our sons when we come to see things the way they really are, and that occurs when we give up our selfish viewpoint and allow God to show us the way.

Just as God is not limited by our cultural norms, men who have surrendered to His influence do not necessarily conform to society's image of a nice guy. Real men don't all look the same and act the same. They share an ability to see things from the vantage point that faith in God provides. The results include hope, love, joy, and a peace that surpasses human understanding. Their relationship with God is dynamic – it impacts their life daily from the inside out, and relationships with people are altered for the better. It enables them to meaningfully touch other people despite differences in culture, occupation, and even language.

Is this the vision of manhood that you learned from your dad, and that you are passing on to your children? It is not a picture of lofty accomplishments and moral perfection. It is a picture of someone **in relationship** – walking closely with God and positively impacting people who are open to being touched by sincere love.

The vision of a real man or man of God that can be derived from what we read in the Old and New Testaments is certainly not related to appearance, social status, income, or accomplishments. It is not a matter of being better or more righteous than someone else. It has a lot more to do with what we think about than our feelings from one moment to the next. Although it allows for widely diverse outcomes in terms of how men live each day, it is characterized as the narrow way (implying that it is impossible to stay on course without God's help).

A Journey of Spiritual Growth

I believe that Scripture gives us distinct principles to consider as we discuss a vision of manhood with our sons. It begins with the decision to enter into a family relationship with God. The family relationship is more intimate than a citizenship relationship where we swear allegiance to the authority of the state and then set out to obey the laws of the state. It is more meaningful than acknowledging the greatness of someone and regularly attending events where that person is recognized.

The family relationship with God involves going where He wants you to go and doing what He wants you to do (of course, because He is your dad and you are His child). Because His motives as a loving father are entirely good, God wants His sons and daughters to mature into adults that reflect His best attributes. We soon learn that in order to "be all that we can be," we really need to "become all that He wants us to become."

> I will be a Father to you,
> and you will be my sons and daughters,
> says the Lord Almighty
> — 2 Corinthians 6:18

Scripture tells us that believers have a **family bond** with God. It's a fact that God the Father adopts you if you accept the adoption process, because you do have a choice. That also makes you an adopted brother or sister of Jesus Christ, who is the only begotten Son of God. It's amazing that, at the same time, God knows us in the way that an ideal father knows his son or daughter, and in the way a mature brother knows his younger sibling.

It is difficult to explain the intensity of God's love for us – a love that drove Him to reduce Himself to human form and then die for us. This is a father's love, and when we learn of it we are invited to accept what Jesus accomplished on our behalf and enter into His family by faith. In doing so we become sojourners on this earth, living for the glory of the Lord and being changed in the process.

Our heavenly father wants to guide us through a process of growing up, from infancy to maturity. Along the way He is observant and protective, yet He allows us the freedom to fail or succeed. He encourages us toward success, and He warns us of danger. He'll be there with us every step of the way, showing us where to go and what to do and how to recognize His presence.

Becoming part of God's family starts us on a journey of spiritual growth which involves an increasing intimacy with Jesus Christ, who together with the Father and Holy Spirit encompasses the fullness of our triune God. Our growth is not primarily about becoming more virtuous – goodness and virtues are important to be sure, but they are byproducts and they are not the foremost goal of our mission.

To grow closer to God, loving Him with all our heart, soul and mind, is our "first and greatest" directive. As He was praying to His Father regarding His present and future followers, Jesus described this intimate relationship as *oneness*.

> I have given them the glory
> that you gave me,
> that they may be one
> as we are one:
> I in them and you in me.
> — John 17:22

The man who walks closely with God becomes less dependent on getting, more deliberate about giving, accepting of himself and his circumstances, secure with his identity in Christ, stronger, more joyful, patient, a real man.

If men and women view one another as brothers and sisters in God's spiritual family, then a level of respect can arise from sincere love toward one another. In particular, we tap into the key strength of all great families: mutual support that stands the test of time.

Our respect for one another includes the recognition that gender is important to family life. Men and women have special roles in the establishment and ongoing success of families, and they are sorely missed when they don't fulfill appropriate roles in family life.

Men are called upon to provide spiritual leadership with a servant's heart, and women are called upon to help family members grow in a supportive but very influential role. There is a "leader-follower" aspect in family life that augments the reality of both spouses as followers (of God) and both spouses as leaders (over their children and in other settings). In the home, men can lead effectively and women can provide appropriate influence if they are both growing in their faith.

If mom and dad are not on the same track spiritually, the situation becomes much more difficult. But one man or woman with sincere faith can still make a difference in any family as they reflect God's love for their spouse and children.

Fathers And Sons Together

Although a healthy parental separation process is part of the boy-to-manhood journey, fathers and sons can remain well connected, particularly with regard to questions of faith and virtues. Even through the teen years, dads can provide spiritual guidance if they take the initiative and if their motivations are sincere.

I have seen many fathers take a vital role in the passing of spiritual life between generations - impacting their own family as well as other families. I have also observed many boys grow to become faithful men of God, influenced in part by dads linking up with each other to face important issues with their sons.

When fathers take the time to focus on the spiritual growth of their sons and to talk and pray with them in the context of a Christian father-son network, profound changes occur in the character development of adolescents.

Hands Outstretched

It was a warm summer evening in Irvine, and I reached over to give my seventeen-year-old son Michael a hug before we got out of the car. The circle of young men gathered on the front lawn in front of Jim's home opened to greet us. It was typical of our gatherings for the boys to be playing and talking outside upon arrival, while we dads assembled within. But this was no ordinary father-son meeting.

No football was being tossed, no basketball was being shot in the driveway, and the greetings were respectful and somber instead of playful. It was an emergency session, if you will, called by my friend Jim in response to the discovery of my son's tumor. This group of men had gathered to participate in a battle against his disease through prayer. These fathers and sons, all of whom knew Michael quite well, were here to encourage us before our trek to USC Norris Cancer Center. These godly men were here to conduct spiritual business.

Michael hung back with the young men while I continued on inside. Strong arms embraced me, one man at a time. I felt weak from lack of sleep (during the past two days my wife Jan and I had been focused on arrangements for surgical removal of the tumor and about one-third of Michael's colon). I also felt weak because my emotions were off the charts. So much for my persona as corporate executive! Enter the broken dad. As is our practice, we fathers talked together before calling our sons in to join us.

Sitting in a circle in Jim's living room, we discussed many issues. These good men wanted to know the details of Michael's condition, the implications of the surgery, and the prognosis for his recovery. How was my wife Jan handling it? How was I holding up? How was our daughter Ina doing? Did we need help getting to or from the hospital? How should they pray?

Then the young men were brought in. Each father addressed Michael as a brother in the family of Christ. They asked caring questions and offered words of encouragement, tender words, and strong words. Then all the fathers and sons gathered around Michael as he stood in the center of the room. They extended their arms, placed their hands on his shoulders and chest, and prayed out loud—tearful petitions, expressions of praise, and statements of thanksgiving for the many evidences of God being at work in Michael's life.

I have no photographs from that night. No digital recording of what was said and done. Yet my mind is full of vivid memories of hands outstretched and men praying boldly. Together, this band of friends and spiritual brothers called upon Michael's heavenly Father for his healing touch.

Michael returned home stronger that night and the ensuing surgery was very successful. He has been cancer-free for many years since that day. There have been other trials along the way, other opportunities for us to grow. Of course, none of us knows what lies ahead on this earth, but we who put our faith in the claims of Jesus Christ do know a few things about our ultimate future—and Michael and I got an early taste of that heaven at Jim's home during the summer of 2004.

Maintaining any relationship takes effort. If fathers assume they will not be able to remain close to their sons during the teen years, then the younger generation is either left on its own or left under the influence of someone else. God has a different game plan – he wants dads to stay involved and make our family connections a priority.

And in the midst of setbacks in those relationships, fathers are still called to love their children. Understanding the special bond between a father and his family is foundational to our faith, to the vibrancy of families, and to the success of communities.

In his book "Faith Begins at Home," Mark Holman refers to the research of George Barna and the Search Institute regarding the interaction between fathers and sons – and, in Mark's words, "we have some serious work to do." The bottom line: only about 5% of fathers have a regular dialog with their teens on faith/life issues. Yet fathers are still ranked high in terms of their influence in the faith of Christian teens (below the influence of mothers but above the influence of friends, other relatives and pastors).

It is important to acknowledge that Christians don't always agree on the practical implications of their faith. After more than a decade of assisting over 100 dads to initiate and maintain father-son groups, I have observed that the wisdom passed from one man to another will vary significantly within each fellowship. Despite the risk of conflicting perspectives that may be difficult to reconcile, these open conversations regarding real life issues are an important part of the journey toward spiritual growth. Young men benefit when they hear various viewpoints from older men who have the same core faith, even if they come from different backgrounds.

The following principles provide a unifying theme for men to contemplate and discuss spiritual growth, while allowing healthy variation in the sharing of experiences regarding manhood:

1. ***Real men don't go along with the world.***
2. ***Real men do what God wants them to do.***
3. ***Real men lead with a servant's heart.***
4. ***Real men build relationships.***
5. ***Real men look beyond this life.***

The website **www.fathersons.org** and the appendices to this book give practical suggestions for organizing group meetings in a way that facilitates discussion and learning (and fun) within a biblical framework, avoids "cookie cutter" formats, and encourages active involvement in each meeting by both fathers and sons.

Questions for Contemplation Or Discussion…

1. How do you relate to God?

There are really two parts of this. Let's call them <u>facts</u> and <u>feelings</u>. On the factual side, how well do you know God and how well does he know you? And in terms of your feelings, do you have a genuine affection toward Him and do you sense that He really likes being with you? Contrary to popular misconceptions of God knowing us "from a distance," God knows us in the way that an ideal father knows his son or daughter, and in the way a mature brother knows his younger sibling. He wants to guide us through a process of growing up, from infancy to maturity. He wants us to see things the way they really are, and that occurs when we give up our selfish viewpoint and allow God to show us the way.

2. What is your vision of a real man, a man of God?

Just as God is not limited by our cultural norms, men who have surrendered to His influence do not necessarily conform to society's image of a nice guy. Real men don't all look the same and act the same. Their relationship with God is dynamic – it changes them daily from the inside out, and their relationships with people are profoundly impacted for the better. The vision of a godly man is not a picture of lofty accomplishments and moral perfection. It is a picture of someone in relationship – walking closely with God and positively impacting people who are open to being touched by sincere love.

2
The Bond between You and God

Our relationship with God is meant to last a long time – well beyond our life on this earth. It's a bond that can bring a genuine sense of contentment to our daily existence here, regardless of circumstances. This key relationship is not about our allegiance to a benevolent yet distant ruler. Although the worldwide scale of God's family is vast and powerful and way over our heads, for you and me it comes down to a personal relationship with God that is intended to be intimate. And that's where the Christian life gets interesting.

How do any of us humans discern and experience a warm and friendly relationship with the triune God of the Bible (Father, Son and Holy Spirit)? Let's start by considering how He has chosen to reveal Himself to us.

The Bible says many things about God, beginning with an account of how He created our world and ending with visions of the establishment of a new heaven and earth. It indicates that God is not of this earth. He is a spirit: a personal being without a physical body (John 4:24). He is one living entity, revealed to us in three persons (Deuteronomy 6:4; Matthew 28:19). He has no limitations to His power and knowledge (Psalm 147:5).

God is eternal: He has always existed, and He always will exist (Psalm 90:2). His attributes don't change (James 1:17). He is good, He is active, and He knows what is best for us (Romans 8:28). God wants us to be people who are capable of loving selflessly and sincerely. In order for that to happen, our heart as well as our view of the world need to be changed, and those changes come—by God's grace and the work of his Spirit—as we grow in our knowledge of Him, and as we actually get to know Him on a personal level.

Knowing and Trusting God

If we accept the truth that God is good—that He truly does have our best interests in mind—and that He is sovereign—that He is in complete control of everything—then we can choose to trust Him and walk in His love. Knowing Jesus is pivotal to our full and accurate understanding of that love. The significance of Jesus in God's unfolding revelation of Himself to mankind cannot be overstated. On the cross, He addressed a fundamental problem that is illustrated almost daily by our failure to choose the right thing when we are given the freedom to choose between right and wrong, good and evil. The cross is a stunning demonstration of love that says "you are family - as important to me as my Son with whom I have been bonded since before time."

> For God so loved the world
> that he gave his one and only Son,
> that whoever believes in him shall not perish
> but have eternal life.
> — John 3:16

How can we comprehend this kind of fatherly love? Some of us did not experience an intimate relationship with our earthly parents during our adolescent years, so it can be hard to take it in. Think for a moment about what we need to do to maintain a relationship with someone. What kinds of things come to mind? Spending time together. Listening to each other. Affirming one another.

Like any relationship that we value, our bond with God needs to be actively sustained by both parties. In the beginning, though, God does what we human beings cannot do: He initiates the relationship. He invites us into His family and adopts us as His sons and daughters (Romans 8:15). God consistently does his part to sustain His relationship with us by being constantly available, unfailing in His love, and, like the perfect Father that He is, providing all that his children need for a purposeful life.

On a spiritual level, He'll show us how to play ball and He'll teach us how to ride a bike. He'll feed us, lead us, pick us up when we fall and hold us in His strong arms when we are afraid. He'll protect us, provide for us and correct us when we get it wrong. He'll find us when we run away and even throw a party for us when we return home. But He doesn't force Himself on us.

Our part in sustaining our relationship with God involves listening to Him and embracing the messages of His love for us that are present in Scripture and that may be conveyed to us by others who are walking closely with Him. An illustration of the importance of listening to Jesus is found in the gospel description of what is called the Transfiguration. Just as Peter is asking a question of Jesus in this mountaintop scene, the Father blesses His Son and expresses a directive for the disciples to hear and record for our benefit.

> While he was still speaking,
> a bright cloud enveloped them,
> and a voice from the cloud said,
> "This is my Son, whom I love;
> with him I am well pleased.
> **Listen to him!**"
> — Matthew 17:5

This gives us a glimpse of the bond of love between God the Father and God the Son. It also gives us the clear instruction to pay attention to what Jesus has to say. In another gospel account, Jesus tells us how it will be possible for you and me to actually listen to Him after His departure from this earth.

> All this I have spoken while still with you.
> But the Counselor, the Holy Spirit,
> whom the Father will send in my name,
> will teach you all things
> and will remind you of everything
> I have said to you.
> — John 14:25-26

For those of us who put our faith in Jesus, the key to growing in our relationship with God involves our daily acquiescence to His indwelling Spirit for guidance and power. However, there is a lingering problem. We often fail to stay on the right spiritual track. It's easy to become discouraged with our shortcomings. If we give up and walk away from God, we will come up with an empty life. If we give up and lean on God even more for the strength to go on, He will show us what forgiveness and renewal are all about.

Listening to the Holy Spirit for Direction

We are able to listen to God when we understand that He speaks not only to mankind in general but to each one of us personally. A vivid Old Testament example of this truth is Elijah's encounter with God described in 1 Kings 17. Elijah received specific directions from the Lord, and "he did what the Lord had told him" (v. 5).

God's directives to people are portrayed as spoken words in Old Testament times, and that may seem awesome or awkward to us. In either case, the fact is that—by his Spirit—God now gets even closer today to people who seek to follow Him and who have been adopted into His family.

> Because you are sons,
> **God sent the Spirit of his Son into our hearts**,
> the Spirit who calls out, "*Abba,* Father."
> So you are no longer a slave, but a son;
> and since you are a son, God has made you also an heir.
> — Galatians 4:6-7

When it comes to our friendship with God, He does the heavy lifting. He takes the initiative; He sets the standards and guides our steps; He has established moral boundaries and is available to help us make wise choices. The key for us—our responsibility—is to stay close to Him in our thought life, to honestly want whatever He wants for us, and to be truly ready to follow His initiative.

> Those who live according to the sinful nature
> have their minds set
> on what that nature desires;
> but **those who live in accordance with the Spirit
> have their minds set on what the Spirit desires**.
> — Romans 8:5

God wants to be first in the hearts of men. When our actions are not rooted in our love for Him, we fall short of our ultimate purpose for living. When what we do reflects a fundamental desire to walk closely with Him, we tend to make better decisions and things seem to fall into place (although they may not be easy or fun at any particular moment). Focusing on God in our thought life is anything but boring. God keeps us moving in a positive direction, and we realize that His direction for our life fulfills our deepest yearnings because He knows us best.

My Work, God's Business

Silence. It would last only about thirty minutes, and I had been given an agenda: to listen and then follow through on what I heard. On that April evening in 1990, my Lord spoke clearly through the silence.

> *It's time to leave your current place of employment. Not a change of profession, but a transition to the kind of workplace where you can be more involved in determining the values that guide executive decisions. You know that this change has already been delayed long enough. Do it now.*

The message, conveyed with authority, was spoken directly to my heart, and it came from a familiar source. At that point in my spiritual journey, I had been a Christian for about seventeen years and I was learning to appreciate the living Word more and more. The Holy Spirit had clearly directed me in many ways, sometimes toward significant life changes.

Learning to recognize the voice of God—to distinguish it from my own inclinations as well as the world's distractions—involves a process of yielding: I learned that, during my quiet times, I needed to express my willingness to follow God and then avoid other distractions. I also learned that during those quiet times I was to focus on prayer, the reading of Scripture, and worship. Then I needed to seek verification from fellow believers whether what I'd thought I heard seemed to be valid (as opposed to my own potentially misguided thoughts). This change-of-workplace message would potentially impact my entire family. So I trusted that my wife Jan would either confirm this idea about changing jobs as a directive from God or challenge me to discern why I came up with such an idea on my own.

The next morning we men gathered to worship together, and then I left for the two-hour drive home. My mind was occupied with the various consequences of leaving my current employer. Would it be possible to fully replace the income I currently enjoyed? I doubted it. Would Jan and I need to sell our home? This seemed quite likely. Thoughts like these soon became prayers, and then, while traveling north on the freeway home, I quietly listened to God. He didn't provide any specific answers, but my anxieties seemed to melt away and be replaced by peace of mind.

At the door of our home, Jan and the kids greeted me warmly with hugs and kisses. As the kids returned to their playthings, Jan and I found ourselves alone for a few minutes.

"Jan, you know how we have always agreed not to hold on too tightly to material things like this house?"

"Yes, of course. Now tell me about your weekend."

As I explained the message I received during my quiet time with God, Jan's response was reassuring and immediate. "Whatever we have to do in terms of our finances and the things we own is fine with me. You clearly need to change employment. When will you give notice?"

"Tomorrow morning."

"Hmmm. OK." A smile. A warm embrace. "Come inside. We missed you."

Two weeks later I was unemployed. A week after that I started a new company with a knowledgeable partner, and it flourished for ten years. In 2000, a new company was born (this time with several partners) - it roared through the up cycle of our economy (peaking in 2006), and has endured the recession that followed. I have worked hard in conjunction with other skilled professionals to develop these enterprises. But since that time alone with God in 1990, I have also seen the hand of the Almighty on these business ventures.

I claim no certainty about the future of our current business, but I am confident that our professional values and goals are appropriate. I also know that God is interested in guiding men and women who face major decisions, including the choice of profession and workplace.

When we let God have a guiding role in our daily life, we are amazed and energized much more often than we feel tired or depressed. And, although life on this earth is never consistently easy, we experience joy even in the midst of difficult circumstances. We are able to say, "Wow! I didn't think I could do that!" rather than "There I go, doing the same wrong thing again." We also know the joy of seeing God work in us and through us, and that experience leaves us humble, grateful, and better able to trust Him as we take the steps He next calls us to take.

> **I have found that
> we can establish ourselves
> in a sense of the presence of God
> by continually talking with Him.**
> It is simply a shameful thing
> to quit conversing with Him
> to think of trifles
> and foolish things.
> — Brother Lawrence, August 3, 1666

So if you are moved to visit someone, to share something, to offer kind words…. to lend a helping hand, to pray silently, to pray out loud with another… to give, to go, to get involved… to learn, to teach, to protect... don't ignore these promptings to do good things.

As you act in these and countless other ways to share God's love with people for His sake, you will learn what true happiness is all about.

Men are also called to openly express our dependence upon God, but that's not easy for us to do. It is easier for many of us to go to a basketball game and shout praises to an athlete whose performance we admire, than to go to church and express our appreciation to Almighty God—our heavenly Father who takes a personal interest in us.

Are we man enough to set aside our pride and worship (adore and revere) the God of the universe with others? He is the only one worthy of such activity.

> Come, let us bow down in worship,
> let us kneel before the Lord our Maker;
> for he is our God and we are the people of his pasture,
> the flock under his care.
> — Psalm 95:6-7

A Prayer for Wisdom

May I remember that you love me
More than I am able to love.

And that your thoughts for me
Are better
Than I could ever imagine.

**My purpose is to follow you
As you accomplish your purposes
Through me.**

To be completely devoted to you, Father
To listen to and obey the words of your Son
To move with your Spirit's guidance
And gather with other souls you have won.

**This day
This moment
I commit myself
To make choices according to your good counsel.**

To love selflessly and sacrificially
as you would have me love.
To walk the path you have for me
Directed from above.

Amen.

Questions for Contemplation Or Discussion…

1. What do you know about God, and how did you learn it?

If you accept the truth that God is good—that He truly does have your best interests in mind—and that He is sovereign—that He is in complete control of everything—then you can choose to trust Him and walk in His love. Knowing Jesus is pivotal to your full and accurate understanding of that love.

2. How can you grow in your relationship with God?

Think for a moment about what you need to do to maintain and build a relationship. We grow closer to God when we allow Him into our daily schedule, when we share our activities with Him, and when we listen to His indwelling Spirit for guidance and power. God wants to be first in the hearts of men. When our actions are not rooted in our love for Him, we fall short of our ultimate purpose for living.

3. Is there room for God in your daily thought life?

Focusing on God in our thought life is anything but boring. God keeps us moving in a positive direction and we realize that His direction for our life fits our deepest needs and fulfills our yearnings because He knows us best. We are amazed and energized more often than we feel tired or depressed. Although life on this earth is never consistently easy, we experience joy even in the midst of difficult circumstances. We are able to say, "Wow! I didn't think I could do that!" rather than "There I go, doing the same wrong thing again."

3
The Brotherhood of Christian Men

Few of us are the jungle explorer types of men. Big spiders and colorful snakes bring out those primal fears that many of us struggle with and that horror films capitalize on. Yet we trek into the wild if family or friends are with us and we have a competent guide and the destination is worth the effort (such as a beautiful waterfall). The "buddy system" is a wise safety measure on land or sea, as well as a great way to share life experiences.

If we are man enough to resist evil in its various forms and break from the ways of the world, then we are probably smart enough to see the importance of getting connected with an active Christian community. It takes effort and risk to form a "band of brothers" around something more than our sporting interests or professional associations, but the benefit in terms of spiritual growth is priceless. Affirmation, learning, and the ability to accomplish more than we could on our own; these are just a few of the reasons men need each other. Will we choose to open up with at least two or three other men who share our values and who will hold us accountable for what we do?

> And let us consider
> how we may spur one another on
> toward love and good deeds.
> Let us not give up meeting together,
> as some are in the habit of doing,
> but let us encourage one another—
> and all the more
> as you see the Day approaching.
> — Hebrews 10:24-25

Purposeful Fellowship

It always amazes me what we learn by actively doing life with other people. They see things we don't see. They know things that we can only learn by being with them when they are ready to share. If we get lost, we can still find our way by connecting with people who know the territory (or who understand how to read the map or operate a GPS device).

Fathers can do so much more to guide their sons and encourage their moral development if we will gather regularly with other dads that share our Christian worldview. Unfortunately we tend to find ourselves driving them from one place to another to drop them off for sports, music practice, church functions, school outings, and many other activities. Even if we stay to watch them perform, this is a distant second to true relationship with them. The outcome of this social blueprint is that our boys will socialize with peers and other adults whom we don't know.

In 1999, a diverse group of us dads (amid the encouragement of our well organized and wise spouses) decided to start meeting once or twice each month with our sons to thoughtfully address topics important to men. The original **F**athers **A**nd **S**ons **T**ogether™ (**FAST**) group spawned the formation of many other such groups at our church and other churches, and along the way these father-son cells have provided encouragement in the midst of many struggles faced by boys and men.

The Schoolyard Bully

The anguish on the father's face got the attention of the other dads even before he said a word. The men had gathered for the usual adult time they enjoyed before inviting their boys in for another father-son fellowship meeting. As the twelve men were settling into the assorted couches and chairs of the church's junior-high room, their eighth-grade sons were playing basketball just outside.

The group leader that night (one of the dads) had been watching each father enter the room and greet the others. He had an agenda for this half-hour window of time, but he set it aside: "Hey, how are you guys doing? Does anyone have something in particular that they would like us to pray about?" The hurting father looked up and realized that his friends were concerned. "I just don't know what to do. My son is being harassed at school by this other kid, and I'm not sure what kind of advice to give him. It has become a real problem."

We've all seen it or even been part of it: one kid hurting another either verbally or physically or perhaps both. This behavior is simply not right, but it is all too common. When it happens over and over again, what is a father's appropriate response? "Welcome to the real world, son." Or "Go tell a teacher about it." Or "Fight back." Or "Just ignore it."

The dads didn't offer quick remedies; instead, they asked questions about this particular situation. Each father knew the son that was being harassed, and after some discussion, they were ready to pray as a group. The prayers for protection, wisdom, and resolution of the problem were spoken with empathy, as though this one son belonged to each and every father there.

When it was time, the boys were brought in, a lesson regarding "resisting peer pressure" was presented, and the sons began to talk with the dads about how to apply the lesson. One of the fathers started to tell a personal story about his encounter with a bully: "When I was in junior high, I had a very difficult time with this big kid who started picking on me for no reason." The harassed son leaned forward with great interest, listened carefully to every detail of the story, and then asked a couple follow-up questions.

That night a harassed son and hurting father went away greatly encouraged. The son learned that strong, godly men had experienced the same thing with which he was struggling. He also learned about adopting strategies to avoid the bully and to focus on building good friendships at school, strategies that the fathers had shared.

Throughout our lives, each of us will face evil in various forms. Although sometimes we feel that we need to face it alone, I believe God is with us. And in many cases the bully— both literally and metaphorically speaking—is best dealt with in community (family and friends). Godly boys and men are called upon to exhibit courage and wisdom, and that wisdom can be gained through fellowship with God and fellowship with his people. Evil too easily prevails when we break these two great circles of fellowship and foolishly set out on our own.

Are there godly men with whom you walk through life, who really know you and your son, and who share your love for God? In society today, men rarely gather to intentionally discuss important life issues, much less to consider deep spiritual questions involving the purpose of our existence and other matters of the soul. That reality has serious consequences for adults, but I think the consequences are even more serious for our sons.

Misconceptions about Friendships

Many misconceptions about friendship exist, so let's separate the myths—the false beliefs and partial truths—from the truth.

Misconception #1: Real men go it alone. This statement is true only in extreme situations when we can't find another person who is seeking God. Yet too many men take on the attitude that they can live life on their own. These men are missing the important truth that they are created by God to be in relationship—with God himself and with God's family, otherwise known as the church. Men are not designed to be self-sufficient: we need friendship because we are designed for community. So the truth is that real men develop friendships, especially with those who share their faith. Since life is a spiritual journey, we can move forward safely and in the right direction only when we have traveling companions who have chosen the same spiritual path.

> If one falls down, his friend can help him up.
> But pity the man who falls
> and has no one to help him up!
> — Ecclesiastes 4:10

Misconception #2: Friendships are all about shared interests. This partial truth often can lead to relationships that are shallow. Furthermore, if sharing an activity together is the only reason for a friendship, then it may actually harm our walk with God.

The mutual commitment to support each other is the mark of true friendship. Finding fun things to do together makes it easier to invest in that friendship, but the fun should not be the only focus. Being real with each other – open, accountable, genuine – gets to the heart of great friendships between men. True friends focus on helping each other succeed, praying for each other, and being available to help with one another's struggles and weaknesses.

> Carry each other's burdens,
> and in this way
> you will fulfill the law of Christ.
> — Galatians 6:2

Misconception #3: Friendships just happen. Many men don't have friends because they don't put forth the effort to make friends. They expect other men to just come alongside them. This lack of effort can lead to an insignificant group of acquaintances and the complete absence of genuine friends.

It takes initiative to have friends who will stand beside you, listen to you, affirm you, and hold you accountable to living a godly life. We therefore need to be deliberate about spending time with other men so we can get to know one another. True friendships occur when we invest time and effort in building relationships that stand the test of time.

It's a serious problem if our closest friends don't relate with our love of God and don't share our desire to grow in a sound biblical understanding of how God wants us to live. When we choose our friends unwisely, the consequences can be disastrous.

> Apples deteriorate…
> Weeds proliferate…
> Disease is contagious…
> Rust corrupts…
> Cancer spreads…
> **And the wrong kind of friends**
> **can kill you.**
> — Stu Weber, Locking Arms

For our sons and daughters I might add that "the wrong kind of girlfriend or boyfriend can kill you," and "the wrong kind of spouse can kill you." Before you enter into these relationships, you need to know that your companion is on the same page with you regarding your Christian faith. You must ask tough questions and be willing to end the relationship if the two of you do not share similar desires to grow closer to God.

On the other hand, this is not an excuse to walk away from marriage vows. If our spouse isn't walking with God as we are, we are called to hang in there and trust that God's love will eventually break through.

Misconception #4: Friends are not to confront each other. Our society values tolerance above all, but the Bible teaches us to speak the truth in love. This involves much more than a bunch of guys hanging out together and having fun. Hanging out together is definitely appropriate for friends, but hanging out is only one aspect of a relationship.

A genuine friendship will at times include confession ("I am in trouble, and I need your help"), while at other times it will call for candor ("You are in trouble, and you need my help").

When confrontation is needed, friends treat one another with sensitivity, but they are also forthright in expressing their concerns regarding errant attitudes or behaviors.

> Better is open rebuke
> than hidden love.
> Wounds from a friend can be trusted,
> but an enemy multiplies kisses.
> — Proverbs 27:5-6

Misconception #5: Your skill at being a friend is measured by how many friends you have. Having a lot of friends does not necessarily indicate how good a friend you can be, but rather that you have an attractive personality, a great sense of humor, giftedness in an activity that other people enjoy, advanced skills that can benefit those around you, or lots of money. True friendship is not measured in numbers.

Instead, genuine friendships are characterized by openness and honesty. Genuine friendships go the distance. Genuine friends are there for one another in times of pain and loss. In fact, the tougher life is, the more we need godly, committed friends.

Each of us needs quality friends, not quantity. We need to be able to anchor our life in a few highly committed relationships.

> A man of many companions may come to ruin,
> but there is a friend
> who sticks closer than a brother.
> — Proverbs 18:24

Relationship Repairs

When misunderstandings happen, or when we deliberately hurt one another and the friendship is fractured, we can sometimes repair the relationship—but not always. We will need to make a choice regarding what we can do on our part to enable both parties to get past the damage. We should not stuff or ignore our hurt feelings and resentment, but we also should avoid talking about these things with everyone around us. As we prayerfully express our feelings to God and allow Him to guide our understanding of what our next steps will be, He ultimately enables us to forgive the person involved.

> He who covers over an offense
> promotes love,
> but whoever repeats the matter
> separates close friends.
> — Proverbs 17:9

This repair process requires us to resist feelings of superiority (instead, we humbly approach the person involved); to accept the pain (we should not set out to hurt the person who hurt us); and to show love when we can do so sincerely (taking the risk that comes with investing in the relationship again).

Such reconciliation is one of the most important and difficult aspects of community life, and there is no guarantee of success because our best efforts may be rejected.

If our efforts to repair a friendship are not successful, we also must be willing to "let go and let God," and allow the friendship to end, at least for a time. Our Lord may well be moving us into a new friendship that otherwise may not have happened.

Praying Together

Prayer is mentioned in the first book of the Bible, it is highlighted in the last book of the Bible, and it is a prominent theme throughout the pages in between. In Revelation we learn that prayer is precious to Jesus and that God receives our prayers as an offering of worship. In the gospels, the prayer life of Jesus teaches the importance of regular, ongoing communion with the Father. In Jesus' parables and later in the epistles, we learn about persevering in prayer, rejoicing in prayer, and joining with fellow believers in prayer.

Prayer may include expressions of our appreciation for God's attributes, openly acknowledging our wrongdoings, committing ourselves to new attitudes and actions, thanking God for divine blessings, and requesting God's help. It also involves our quiet reflection as we listen to what God may be saying to us.

Although prayer is conversing with God and not with other people, prayers spoken out loud to God in a gathering of believers are powerful faith-builders and result-getters. When fathers and sons agree together in prayer, they can expect to see God work in mighty ways.

> "Again, truly I tell you that if two of you on earth
> agree about anything they ask for,
> it will be done for them
> by my Father in heaven.
> **For where two or three gather in my name,**
> **there am I with them."**
> — Matthew 18:19-20

Prayer is an amazing privilege: God has chosen to allow his people to have a meaningful role in accomplishing his goals on this earth and for our lives. Our prayers and His will mysteriously work together for His glory and our good. When we pray, we are not controlling God's actions or manipulating His power. Instead, when we pray, we are expressing our dependency on Him, and we submit ourselves to His perfect will.

We effectively connect with God in prayer when we approach Him with genuine remorse for our sins, renewed commitment to living in compliance with His ways, unreserved devotion and trust in Him, acceptance of His forgiveness, and clear thinking.

> You will seek me and find me
> when you seek me with all your heart.
> — Jeremiah 29:13

Accountability and Purity

As today's smart phone apps, internet sites, books, magazines, movies, television, and music indicate, our society celebrates sex outside of marriage. Our culture also promotes sex and materialism in the name of freedom, but the motives are much darker than that. Author C. S. Lewis put it this way: "There are people who want to keep our sex instinct inflamed in order to make money out of us. Because, of course, a man with an obsession is a man who has very little sales-resistance."

Real men understand the power of sexual attraction and work together to resist the temptations to view pornography and to get involved in sexual activity outside of marriage. When godly men do stumble, they confess their sins to God first and then also to each other, so that they can pray for one another and get back on track.

> Therefore confess your sins to each other
> **and pray for each other**
> **so that you may be healed**.
> The prayer of a righteous man
> is powerful and effective.
> — James 5:16

Because God created men to be so visual, how can we resist sexual temptations? To find success in this struggle, we need to be realistic about our own limitations and know where our weaknesses lie. For example, my friends and I pray specifically for each other when we travel (access to adult videos and being alone in a hotel room are a dangerous combination), holding one another accountable by asking questions and being willing to answer each other truthfully. My son Michael has made similar arrangements with his friends.

The Hill Cries Out

At first Jan and I didn't quite know what to make of it. Michael had come home at about 10:00 p.m. with three of his friends, grabbed his guitar, and headed out again into the night. "Hey, Mom and Dad! We're going to the hill to talk and pray and sing. I'll be home by midnight."

When I was Michael's age, my buddies and I didn't typically go to a lonely lookout spot to worship God! Oh, Michael was well aware of the normal temptations of teenage life, but he had a certain maturity that I claimed only when I was much older. Also, most of his friends—many of whom I had come to know very well—shared his love of God.

So Jan and I shrugged our shoulders, we offered our usual warning ("Be safe, don't disturb anyone, and watch out for one another"), and Michael's band of brothers headed to the hillside trail near our home. Jan and I headed to bed, but sleep would evade us until our "young adult" son was back in his bedroom.

After all, Michael had gotten into mischief with his buddies before, but fortunately those adventures tended to be harmless— although some of their water-balloon launching escapades did cause some damage. But our parental intuitions told us that their worship times on the hill near our house were sincere and special. Michael was a bit resistant to our curiosity regarding exactly what these guys were talking about, so we settled for praying for them while they hiked up the hill to pray and sing into the night.

The truth about some of those worship times, however, slipped out a couple years later. Michael and I were having a frank talk about our struggles as men to avoid the temptations that bombard us through the media and via the Internet. It turns out that a couple of his friends in our father-son group had made a pact together: "When fighting temptation, let's get out in nature and worship and pray and confess and encourage one another." And that's what some of their prayer times on the hill were all about—and that is spiritual power. The community of believers in action. Real-life godliness.

I wonder how many neighbors may have heard these young men singing as they worshipped at the top of the hill. We have coyotes living in these hillsides, and at night we sometimes hear their whining cries. But the sound from Michael and his friends would have been a very different sound, the holy and heavenly sound of young men crying out to God for forgiveness and strength. It was not just howling at the moon (although occasionally there may have been some of that thrown in…).

One of the keys to living a pure life seems rooted in how we think about things, how we prepare ourselves to resist evil, and how we proactively enter into the positive activities that God calls us to.

> Set your minds
> on things above,
> not on earthly things.
> — Colossians 3:2

God does not want us to be a slave to earthly attractions. He wants us to appreciate true beauty and to experience true joy. The fulfillment of our sexual desires in marriage is a naturally good thing, and completely in line with what is right in God's eyes. If we choose to act according to our sexual desires outside of marriage, however, we enter a dangerous realm where desires are never really fulfilled and relationships are damaged. While sex within a marriage relationship reinforces family life, sex outside of marriage distorts and violates family life.

Sharing a Good Thing with Everyone

Christians have good reason to get out of themselves and build honest, uplifting relationships with people around them. If our concerns for the welfare of others are genuine, then of course we will not shy away from discussing our relationship with God. Friends or colleagues may or may not want to listen to what we have to share, but first we must overcome some of our own insecurities about discussing spiritual matters. We have many reasons for sharing our faith, but too often our own concerns about "doing it right" keep us from doing anything at all, and we find ourselves being quiet about how God has changed our life. We don't, for instance, want to insult anyone or say something that is politically incorrect. We may worry about the potential hostility of others, and hostility is indeed a possible response.

But another reason we hesitate to share our faith may be a lack of motivation: we may be out of touch with the spiritual needs of the people around us. We sometimes forget how listless our spirit was before our own personal encounter with the life-changing love of God.

Also complicating our attempts to share our faith is the reality that many people confuse Christianity with religion. The Christian faith is actually a personal relationship with the living God, not an institution. Are we letting them get close enough to us so that they can see that? The relationships we experience in our fellowship with

God and with other believers are the kinds of relationships that anyone should be attracted to, but how often do we invite others to join in?

Finally, we need to be aware that our partial awareness of the views of the people around us should not lead us to think that we know what they are thinking. We don't know what God is doing in their lives. We should sincerely respect them, and we should also be willing to talk about our relationship with the Lord, to invite them to join us in Christian fellowship activities, to ask their permission to pray out loud for them if the circumstances merit that, and to not be upset if they say no to any of these things. Our outreach is not about us: it's all about God, and He certainly makes it possible for men and women and children to find Him if they look for Him.

> But if from there you seek the LORD your God,
> you will find him
> if you look for him with all your heart
> and with all your soul.
> — Deuteronomy 4:29

Outreach is not about our need to perform in a certain way, to eloquently speak God's truth, or to have all the answers to difficult questions about God. Outreach is about having a heart for people in need, whether the stranger, the poor person, the addict, the painfully shy person, the janitor, or the associate who turned on us. Outreach is about loving people with God's active and compassionate love.

> "Lord, when did we see you hungry and feed you,
> or thirsty and give you something to drink?
> When did we see you a stranger and invite you in,
> or needing clothes and clothe you?
> When did we see you sick or in prison
> and go to visit you?"
> The King will reply, "I tell you the truth,
> whatever you did for one of the least
> of these brothers of mine, you did for me."
> — Matthew 25:37-40

As Christians, we have made the decision to receive from our Lord the amazing gifts of forgiveness for our sins, the ability to be in relationship with the God of the universe, and eternal security in Him. We were able to make this decision because of the truths communicated to us in the Bible and because of the work of the Holy Spirit within us, through other people, and in the world God created.

Each of us receives God's truth in a unique and personal way, and He continues to communicate His truth in countless ways and various cultural settings. In obedience to God's command to share His truth with others, godly men are open to discussing rival concepts of God. We don't, however, accept the notion that "it doesn't matter what you believe as long as you have faith in something and live a good life." The object of our faith is important because it is true or false, real or fake. And eternity hangs in the balance.

> If there is a God,
> you are, in a sense, alone with Him.
> You cannot put Him off
> with speculations about your next door neighbors
> or memories of what you have read in books.
> What will all that chatter and hearsay count
> (will you even remember it?)
> when the anesthetic fog which we call
> "nature" or "the real world" fades away
> and the Presence in which you have always stood
> becomes palpable, immediate, and unavoidable?
> — C. S. Lewis, *Mere Christianity*

What we believe and what others believe is important, and we who follow Jesus should be willing to discuss such important matters. Our attitude when we do so should be humble: we didn't invent our faith, and we don't know how or when God will open a person's heart to His truth. We are to simply share what we know: we have encountered Jesus; his message of love, forgiveness, and grace is awesome; and we want other people to check it out for themselves.

Questions for Contemplation Or Discussion...

1. Do you have a core group of Christian friends who know you and your family?

It takes initiative to have friends who will stand beside you, listen to you, affirm you, and hold you accountable. True friendships occur when we invest the time and effort - when we are open and honest with one another, and actively pursue a closer walk with God together.

2. How do you feel about praying with other Christians?

Although prayer is talking to God and not to other people, prayers spoken out loud to God in a gathering of believers are powerful faith-builders and result-getters. When men agree together in prayer, they can expect to see God work.

3. Because God created men to be so visual, how can we resist sexual temptations?

Real men understand the power of sexual attraction and work together to resist it. When godly men do stumble, they confess their sins to God first and then also to each other, so that they can pray and get back on track.

4. What's my role in expanding the brotherhood of Christian fellowship?

If we are honest and sincere, willing to both share information and listen to the views of others, opportunities will arise. Godly men are always open to discussing rival concepts of God. We don't, however, accept the notion that "it doesn't matter what you believe as long as you have faith in something and live a good life."

4
Marriage and Family

My friend was earnest in his request to meet for lunch. "John, I need to talk with you, and it's important." He was 10 years younger than me, married with two young children. We had recently gotten to know one another in a men's bible study group. After the normal greeting and ordering of food, he leaned in close to the table. "My marriage is in trouble. Perhaps it's the strain of raising the kids, but our sex life has become non-existent and we aren't being kind to one another. In any case, I don't think I love my wife anymore. To top it off, there's this woman at work who really likes me, and I'm starting to have feelings for her."

"Have you acted on those feelings?"

"No. That's why I wanted to meet. I need real help with this right now, or things are going to get out of control soon."

I was so proud of this younger man – his intentionality to work on the matter was sincere. My wife Jan and I had already seen two marriages fall apart in our circle of friends. In each case there was not a serious attempt by the man involved to work through tough issues. They had "lost that loving feeling" and divorce was the easy way out.

"Have you been courting your wife during this past year?"

"What do you mean?"

"Date nights, dinners out (with babysitters you have arranged), movies, surprises that just say 'I love you.'"

"No. I don't feel that way for her."

"Have you considered that these things don't need to be motivated by your feelings? When we do things because they are the right things to do, sometimes we're rewarded with the generation of new feelings of love and intimacy. Even if it takes a long time, I can tell you from experience that it's well worth the effort."

"What if the feelings don't come?"

"I will just about guarantee that your love for her will be there if you will pursue her, dating her weekly, expressing your commitment to her daily, and honestly seeking God's view of the matter during the next few months. At the same time, you need to stay away from any personal relationship with this other woman at work."

"John, are you serious? Have you been dating Jan that often during your 20 years together?"

"Absolutely. And my feelings of love for Jan are even more intense than our first year of marriage. We have experienced some very difficult seasons in our relationship, but I'm glad we stayed the course. You will be too. Let's continue to meet together and I will hold you accountable to do this."

That lunch meeting occurred 15 years ago. Today my friend is more mature, his marriage is strong, and their children have grown up. It took several months back in 1995 for his feelings to return, and there were bumps in the road which he and his wife have traveled together during the years that followed, but now they are reaping the many rewards of a long term relationship. Jan and I are also enjoying the relational benefits of 35 years together. Others have missed out on so much because they let their feelings take them astray and terminated their marriage without aggressively struggling over an extended period of time to keep it.

Healthy Marriages Thrive with Servant Leaders

Our feelings are not to control our actions, especially when it comes to building and nourishing a healthy marriage and being a servant-leader in our home.

The idea that "being in love"
is the only reason for remaining married really leaves no room
for marriage as a contract or promise at all.
If love is the whole thing, then the promise can add nothing;

and if it adds nothing, then it should not be made.
A promise must be about things that I can do, about actions:
**no one can promise to go on feeling a certain way.
He might as well promise
never to have a headache or always to feel hungry.**
— C. S. Lewis, *Mere Christianity*

Deciding to love is more wondrous than falling in love. After the wedding day, we cultivate romance by being a good friend to our wife and by continuing to court or date her. Whenever you lose that loving feeling (and all of us will from time to time), the solution is to take action—to work at the relationship—rather than simply allowing the two of you to drift further apart or blaming your spouse for the waning of your feelings.

As a servant leader, the husband is to honor and pray for his wife, consider her interests ahead of his own, and not hurt her with unkind words or deeds. He is to cultivate a deeper love relationship with her by investing in their marriage.

The commitment to be faithful in marriage should impact all of our relationships, and we should be especially careful about how we relate to other women. When a man gets married, he becomes a one-woman man. He needs to take great care to handle innocent encounters with women wisely, so that there is not the appearance of a weakened commitment or any hint of wrong intentions. Of course married men also respond to the God-given call to be compassionate to any woman in need and to have healthy friendships and/or professional relationships with women. However, we are to guard against these relationships becoming too personal – our deepest feelings should be shared with our wife.

**Marriage should be honored by all,
and the marriage bed kept pure,**
for God will judge the adulterer
and all the sexually immoral.
— Hebrews 13:4

Men have special roles in the establishment and ongoing success of families, and they are sorely missed when they don't fulfill their roles. Misunderstandings about the spiritual leadership of men in our homes are rampant. Sometimes they arise from a warped view of leadership that says leaders are ambitious and selfish, seeking to rule instead of serve. The words of Jesus as well as his lifestyle paint a clear picture of godly leadership that combines guidance with love and direction with selfless motives. The Bible challenges men to step up and guide their family in a close walk with God—and women to support them to accomplish this goal.

It's no surprise that the best "how to" guide for marriage—and any relationship—is found in God's Word. We learn that loving another person involves an exchange: our strength goes out, and the other person's weakness comes in. We decrease so that someone else can increase. We sacrifice some of our freedom so they can gain freedom. This is the "substitution effect" of love in marriage, modeled for us by God's love (and demonstrated by Christ's sacrificial love for the church).

> **Love is patient, love is kind.**
> It does not envy, it does not boast,
> it is not proud. It is not rude,
> it is not self-seeking, it is not easily angered,
> it keeps no record of wrongs.
> Love does not delight in evil but rejoices with the truth.
> **It always protects, always trusts,**
> **always hopes, always perseveres.**
> — 1 Corinthians 13:4-7

If men and women view one another as brothers and sisters in God's spiritual family, then a level of respect can arise from sincere love toward one another. If we haven't already learned it from the challenges of living with people, we certainly learn from Scripture that forgiveness is at the heart of any meaningful relationship. It's important to forgive and it's important to accept forgiveness from others.

Where Are You Needed Most?

I love to work on projects. Defining the problem, evaluating possible solutions, and working toward a successful outcome within a given schedule—these are things I do best. I love the challenge of working to meet a deadline so that I can complete one project and then begin another. I also work well in the context of partnerships and boards where I can help define goals and then determine how best to achieve those goals.

In sharp contrast to being an executive in the business world, being a dad is not about projects that begin and end and operate on my schedule. Instead, fatherhood is all about process and people, about my spouse and our children, and about addressing needs that change day by day. But I initially thought that I could become a successful father without changing my project-oriented approach to life. I was wrong....

One evening in 1989, God taught me a valuable lesson. On this occasion, He spoke through the words of my wife (an event that has happened many times). Her loving but firm words were revealed in a profound question: "Where do you think you are needed most tonight?"

It had been a busy day at the office. My profession as a transportation planning consultant requires frequent interaction with public officials and private developers on important infrastructure issues, and the work is stressful. I had come home drained of energy, and I only had about forty-five minutes to spend with my family before leaving to attend a church board meeting. I considered my role as a church elder to be a high calling, and several decisions involving ministry priorities and facility plans needed to be made that night at the meeting.

Within moments of my arrival at home, though, it became apparent that Jan was also drained of energy. The profession of homemaker requires constant interaction with children, especially before they enter grade school. In 1989, Ina was five years old and Michael was an active two-year-old. Jan had prepared a home-cooked meal, and the four of us ate a hurried dinner together. Michael was more than ready for some time with Dad, but I was already thinking about the board meeting that would soon begin. As I walked out the door, Jan had just one simple question: **"Where do you think you are needed most tonight?"**

That question did not stop me from leaving the house, but it took center stage in my thoughts as I drove to church. "Lord, am I doing the right thing by putting this meeting first?"

> *John, you need to recognize that your involvement in church leadership also happens to be something you enjoy doing. Fatherhood stretches you, so you focus on other things. That should end tonight. While your children are young, you need to prioritize family life and stay involved with your kids*

The Lord opened my eyes to many things during that short drive. I realized that I was at risk of missing the time-sensitive opportunity of being a good father. I saw that I needed to change my project-first orientation and put people first, especially when it came to my family. I also recognized that, at this phase of life, given the needs of my spouse and children as well as other responsibilities and commitments, evenings with my son and daughter were precious and not to be minimized or wasted.

I had served as an elder for a six-year period that included some difficult pastoral staff transitions. Other men had recently answered the call to leadership at our church. I explained to them that God was calling me to redirect my priorities. They accepted and affirmed my decision to leave the board that very night.

Jan had spoken truth to me in the form of a question and God spoke clearly as I contemplated her words. Often God uses those who love us most to challenge our thinking and get us on the right path.

God calls us to work, and He blesses our work when we do it as unto Him. But we should not let our work become our top priority. As we purchase and accumulate things, we need to keep in mind the truth that God ultimately owns everything we have. We are stewards of what is actually the Lord's; we are managing his property. How men spend their time and how they spend their money significantly impacts the health of their marriage and vitality of their family. God gives us only certain amounts of time and money to allocate between various activities – will we spend these limited resources wisely?

Family Finances

There are basically three appropriate uses of money, and we should be involved in all three concurrently.

- First, God provides us with money so that we can provide our families through responsible spending, paying bills on time, wise saving for retirement and emergencies, and for self-improvement (including education and recreation).

- Second, God wants us to use money to help those in need, and to support the infrastructure of society. We do that by paying taxes, giving to the poor, and sharing with others.

- Third, God gives us money to invest in his kingdom. We make such an investment when we give to the local church, when we support Christian ministries that serve throughout the world, and when we finance our own ministry activities.

Unwise uses of money include overindulging, wasteful spending, reaching beyond our means, and hoarding or storing away money in ways that yield no benefit to anyone. Although money and possessions generally represent the fruit of our labor, we should also acknowledge that we temporarily have such things because of God's grace. If we are not careful about how we handle money, we can find ourselves in debt or even bankrupt and working just to pay off our debts instead of being able to provide generously for our family.

> For the love of money is a root of all kinds of evil.
> Some people, eager for money,
> have wandered from the faith
> and pierced themselves with many griefs.
> — 1 Timothy 6:10

If we love money too much—if we love it more than we love God or people—then that love will ultimately destroy us as we pursue money at all costs rather than the relationships that he created us for. The compulsive pursuit of money can become as addictive as alcohol or drug abuse, consuming our daily activities and ruining our health. If, however, we acquire and use money wisely, it simply becomes a means of greater and more effective stewardship.

Capitalizing on Contentment

It is important to God that, even as we work hard, we enjoy a sense of contentment, that feeling of calm satisfaction that comes from living within our means and not craving more than we can afford. So what can we do to resist spending more than we earn? The answer to that question is nothing mysterious or unique. Simply establish a personal budget for your monthly activities. Decide before the money comes in how much you will save, how much you will give to the needy and to God's work through his church, and how much you will spend on food, clothing, transportation, rent or mortgage, utilities, education, travel, entertainment and (of course) taxes. Write down your budget, keep track of how much you actually spend, and see how you do each month. Adjust your spending so that you stay within your budget.

Another key to resisting the desire to spend more than you earn is to only use a credit card if you can pay it off each month—before you are charged any interest. The moment you are charged interest because you can't keep up on payments, eliminate the credit card and use cash, checks, or a debit card only. Then limit your spending of money, and instead spend more time with the Lord and your wife and your children and others (instead of spending your way into debt).

> I know what it is to be in need,
> and I know what it is to have plenty.
> **I have learned the secret of being content
> in any and every situation**,
> whether well fed or hungry,
> whether living in plenty or in want.
> — Philippians 4:12

If you advance in your career, you will need to decide when enough is enough. If you are blessed with plenty, at some point you should stop pursuing an ever larger home and fancier cars. If you have more than you need (and you should prayerfully consider what that means for your family), then enjoy giving away what God has blessed you with as he directs you through this brief life on earth.

Questions for Contemplation Or Discussion...

1. Why is it difficult for men to step up and guide their family in a close walk with God?

Misunderstandings about the spiritual leadership of men in our homes are rampant. This kind of leadership involves modeling a daily walk with God in words and deeds, being a good provider, handling money responsibly, loving sincerely, and maintaining a healthy marriage. It also involves a commitment to do with excellence whatever God has called us to do, and to forgive each other when we fail.

2. What is the "root of all kinds of evil" and at the epicenter of many broken marriages?

Love of money distorts our priorities and inhibits our generosity because it is inherently self-centered. Those who love money end up alone, relationally bankrupt. It is important to God that, even as we work hard, we enjoy a sense of contentment, that feeling of calm satisfaction that comes from living within our means and not craving more than we can afford.

3. Why should I stay in a marriage if we have fallen out of love with each other?

"I don't feel like it" is never an acceptable reason to not love another person. Our feelings are not to control our actions, especially when it comes to building and nourishing a healthy marriage. Whenever you lose that loving feeling (and all of us will), the solution is to take action—to work at the relationship—rather than simply allowing the two of you to drift further apart.

5
A Heart for the Next Generation

New fathers will sometimes ask older and presumably wiser parents this basic question: "Is there a right way to raise my kids?" Too often the response will be "Just love them as best you can - there is no right way and once your children reach the teen years they will stop listening to you anyway." In the debate of "nature vs. nurture," many frustrated parents have given up on their ability to influence their kids because they are disappointed with the outcome of their own nurturing efforts, and/or they are confounded by the unique personalities their kids were born with.

I believe that there are thoughtful and substantive answers to the "how to raise my kids" question, which build upon the "love them well" theme with many useful steps we can take along the way. We are not guaranteed that our adult children will make good decisions as they mature, but parents who are willing to look back humbly on the way they raised their kids can often identify mistakes they made and discern a better course of action. Insights into fatherhood can also be gained by evaluating the current routines we fall into as we "do life" together as a family.

> A simple man believes anything,
> but a prudent man gives thought to his steps.
> — Proverbs 14:15

Self evaluation is healthy as long as it is constructive and enables us to move forward, forgiving ourselves and perhaps seeking forgiveness from family members if appropriate. Jan and I have sought the forgiveness of our children at several points along their journey to adulthood, and it has contributed to healing and restoration. Here are five questions that give support to this process:

1. Are we cultivating a bond of genuine affection with our children?

2. Do we have a consistent and loving approach to discipline?

3. Are we openly discussing spiritual growth issues?

4. Is our family involved in a community that shares our faith and values?

5. Are we attentive to our own health as well as the health and well being of our children and our spouse?

Relationship Time: Quantity AND Quality

Most dads want to have a good relationship with their sons and daughters, but not every dad invests the time and intentionality that is needed. Each child needs individual time with dad, one-on-one, as well as group time with siblings and friends and other parents, but dads should not expect their kids to take the initiative. Great relationships between fathers and their children can only occur if dads are proactive and set the stage for meaningful interaction.

It begins by seizing opportunities to know who your children are, while at the same time enabling them to know who you are. It's also important that they come to know your friends, and that you get to know their friends as well.

All relationships involve a process of revealing bits and pieces of who we are, even as we come to understand the attitudes and feelings of other people. One of the ways that we reveal ourselves to each other is by talking together. Our conversations disclose something of our character traits, interests and world view. The commitment to a genuine relationship with our children will therefore consist of both being with them and conversing with them.

Fathers should become adept at the art of conversation, which involves asking and answering questions in ways that enable a fluid exchange of ideas. We all know the frustration of asking open ended questions to people who are difficult to build a rapport with, only to receive one word responses (also known as "conversation killers"). When possible, answer your son's question with a balanced response that reveals your perspective but doesn't become a lecture. And ask questions that invite your son to share something of what he knows and feels.

Getting a Handle on Discipline

When children disobey or choose dangerous, unhealthy paths, fathers need to respond wisely. God calls us to act with appropriate authority and guidance, and the specifics of the situation will help us determine what is appropriate. Too often, however, we either ignore the problem (and this usually doesn't help our children), or we respond with unrighteous anger - and that's an issue we need to deal with before it becomes a problem that complicates the original act of disobedience.

> A fool gives full vent to his anger,
> but a wise man keeps himself under control.
> — Proverbs 29:11

Discipline Scenario #1

Let's begin with an easy example. (At least it should be easy, but many of us struggle with it mightily.) Your son makes a mistake. He didn't know that if he did *this* thing, then *that* bad thing would result. Something gets broken, or someone gets hurt.

The appropriate response is **instruction**: we provide—formally or informally—either spoken or written directives of what must be done and why. We combine this instruction with **training**, with the patient repetition of that instruction over time in order to improve our son's understanding. Inappropriate responses include degradation

("You idiot!"), rejection ("Get out of here!"), or avoidance of the issue altogether.

> A man's wisdom gives him **patience**;
> it is to his glory to overlook an offense.
> — Proverbs 19:11

Discipline Scenario #2

This second example addresses disobedience resulting from a lack of self-control. Your son, for instance, knows full well that he shouldn't run through the living room, but "he can't help himself."

The appropriate response is **correction**: you call for a change in your son's activity and offer consequences for the poor choice he made. You stop the activity, require an explanation and apology to the offended party, arrange for a time-out, enforce consequences that were established earlier, or set restrictions on certain privileges. Inappropriate responses include personal attack or ridicule ("You obviously can't control yourself!"), unrighteous anger (striking or slapping because of our own irritation or resentment), or enforcing no consequences at all because you have been worn down and exhausted by the relentlessness of parenting.

> Discipline your son, and he will give you peace;
> he will bring delight to your soul.
> — Proverbs 29:17

Discipline Scenario #3

The final example involves our son's rejection of our authority. (This kind of disobedience may occur when we have not addressed the issues discussed above, or it may be related to his temperament, as I'll discuss below.) Our son knows he is not allowed to leave without telling us where he is going, but he does it anyway. Maybe he's attempting to establish or assert his freedom to do whatever he pleases, or perhaps his disobedience is a cry for attention. Attentive parents can determine the difference between their son's lack of self-control and his deliberate acts of rebellion.

Before proposing an appropriate response, let me offer you some insights that may be helpful. First, the same approaches to discipline don't yield the same responses in every child. Don't panic—but also don't give up. Sound approaches to training your child will prove effective if you remain consistent. Is your will as strong as his will? You may need to say "no" many more times. He may continue to push against the boundaries you've established. Do you love him enough to take on this challenge? Also, consider whether your son is trying to tell you something through his misbehavior. Make that—like any situation calling for discipline—a topic of prayer.

A brief aside: Some parents don't have any children who are strong willed, and these parents will tell you that strong discipline is never needed if you train your children correctly. Consider the limitations of their viewpoint - these parents probably just don't understand the measures needed to address children that repeatedly challenge authority.

Now let me offer an appropriate response to your son's disrespectful disobedience: Stay connected with him. Let him see that you respect him. Tell him that you love him – say those words out loud. Also, when your son is young (less than twelve years old) and his behavior calls for it, you and your spouse should consider using appropriate and respectful physical consequences when your intention is to put him back on the right path. You and your spouse should determine the age-appropriate consequences that you both can realistically and consistently implement.

> **Do not withhold discipline** from a child;
> if you punish him with the rod, he will not die.
> Punish him with the rod and save his soul from death.
> — Proverbs 23:13-14

Avoid punishment in public: do not embarrass or humiliate your son. Avoid responding to disobedience out of anger; exercise self-control and be sure your motives are pure. Take your son to a private place. This gives you a moment to pray and "cool off" before you issue punishment. Then bring closure to the situation with a sincere expression of your love and a heartfelt reminder that you are committed to your son's well being. And be certain that your son fully understands how to make better choices and avoid punishment in the future.

Inappropriate responses by you to disrespectful disobedience include any angry reactions that are rooted in your own selfish needs or desires. Be aware of when you are on edge and not able to think clearly about the incident. Remember that striking your son or slapping him because you are irritated, angry, or resentful is not appropriate. (In fact, a slap on the face is disrespectful.) Often we need to step away for a moment, catch our breath, and regain control of ourselves. I also strongly encourage you to pick your battles wisely. And know that, with God's leading, you can win this fight for the character development of your child. Don't surrender to discouragement - enlist the prayer support of other men and women who love your son, and stay engaged. Your son's development as a man of God is definitely worth fighting for!

Passing Along a Unique Perspective

When we consider the vision of maturity we desire to openly discuss with our family, it is certainly not "outward religion." For the Christian, spiritual growth is all about inner change that transforms each of us from the inside out. The faith we want our sons to embrace is an authentic relationship with God which comes to life in the context of a continual journey with Christ.

Christians believe that God has provided a way of forming a personal relationship with Him that involves acknowledgement of shortcomings, forgiveness of wrongdoings through his grace, and changes to actions that flow from the work of the Holy Spirit. His method (sending his Son to earth) was difficult for many people to accept when it occurred 2000 years ago, and that remains so today.

The fact that men and women could be made right with God, which includes the acknowledgment that they can't be good enough to save themselves and that Jesus Christ fulfilled the requirements of God's righteousness on their behalf, challenged prevailing religious norms and also challenged Roman authority (that required worship of their deities and the emperor). Because this message of grace and forgiveness and freedom calls for men to trust in Christ, He becomes a focal point that must be discussed with their sons.

Healthy viewpoints on goodness, self-control, brotherly kindness, and love are shared with many philosophies and religions around the world. However, Christian fathers who have experienced God's grace have much more to share with their sons than good values. They can model and share a vital relationship with God. This active relationship enables boys and men to break free from hindrances and live with a new standing before God that is filled with hope.

Involvement in a Faith Community

Someone will influence your son; someone other than you. So do you know the interests and the hearts of boys and girls he is spending time with? Do you know the parents of his friends? Perhaps even more important, does your son know any other Christian fathers? And do any other fathers really know your son? A fellowship of men who trust in God is important in a boy's growth and development. That kind of fellowship is also important for us dads and all of our family members. It contributes to our spiritual maturity and greatly affects the type of person each of us will become, inside and out.

> He who walks with the wise
> grows wise,
> but a companion of fools suffers harm.
> — Proverbs 13:20

One reason we may not know our son's friends is that men often let our own social life be centered on our work connections or on acquaintances who share our interest in a specific sport or hobby. It's all too easy to fall into this pattern and miss out on relationships that go beyond work and sports. Fathers can make a difference by purposefully choosing to connect their family with a church community that includes other families who are pursuing the God of the Bible.

We can best help our sons and daughters make wise choices when we share a support system for living in a way that honors God. This occurs when we spend time with others who have faith in Jesus that is genuine, who have hope that is energized by his Spirit, and who put into practice the love of God. As part of our God-given responsibilities, we fathers also need to think logically about practical things that impact the health and well being of our family members.

Personal Health

Eating healthy food, exercising daily or at least weekly, getting an appropriate amount of rest, developing an appreciation of music, and reading – these are personal disciplines that a father should reinforce for both himself and his family.

OK, nutrition and physical activities and relaxation are basic priorities for healthy people, but you may be asking "why are music and books also priorities for my well being?" I have found that the healthiest people I know really enjoy music and also read for leisure or to learn. They sing when they are having fun with others, they listen to wholesome music for encouragement and perspective, and they enjoy reading good books and discussing what they are learning with their friends. When Jan and I gather with our friends and/or family, music and talking about things we have read are inevitably part of our experience of being together.

Some men may object to music as a life priority because they can't carry a tune or catch a rhythm. I'm not suggesting that we need to develop proficiency for music performance in order to have a healthy lifestyle. Men who can't sing on key are still able to bring good music into their home or take their family to uplifting musical performances.

Back to the basics: let's examine food for a moment. Eating is so much more than a basic requirement for our survival. It is an activity that often becomes the focus of obsessive behaviors, so we need to handle it with care. Modern methods of food processing and distribution provide ample opportunity for consumption of things that harm us. Our appetites may become addictions, and then our bodies suffer the consequences.

The key words for nutrition are "variety" and "moderation." On a daily basis, we need an appropriate mix of vitamins, protein, carbohydrates and fats from vegetables, fruits, seeds, nuts, beans, grains and meats. And we need water as well. If we don't have a steady diet that encompasses most of these things, then supplements (nutrient rich powders or capsules) may help to fill the gap.

Our bodies are built to move, and physical activities that stretch our muscles and require them to keep working will yield many benefits (including easier management of our eating habits). For example, one way for fathers to avoid unhealthy nighttime routines (snacking or excessive TV) is to regularly take an evening walk with their spouse and other family members.

A good friend of mine and his wife have walked together daily throughout most of their 35 years of married life, and discovered that a key benefit is the bonding time it affords (talking and listening to each other while exercising).

Rest is equally important to diet and exercise, but we must be disciplined to accomplish it in healthy ways. Staying up too late at night can impact our ability to get through the following day, so we need to look ahead and schedule our sleep intervals. Reading can help us slow down and prepare our mind and body for sleep.

When men don't pay attention to their health, the consequences can be severe. Appetites become bad habits and addictions which then have a ripple effect of emotional and physical harm to themselves as well as their loved ones. The causes of addiction are complex, but mature men are able (by the grace of God) to stay healthy in the areas of life that they can control.

God, grant us the...
Serenity to accept things we cannot change,
Courage to change the things we can,
and the Wisdom to know the difference.
— Reinhold Niebuhr

Questions for Contemplation Or Discussion...

1. Are you cultivating a bond of genuine affection with your children?

Fathers should become adept at the art of conversation, which involves asking and answering questions in ways that enable a fluid exchange of ideas.

2. Do you and your spouse have a consistent and loving approach to discipline?

Appropriate responses to unwise choices and bad behaviors include instruction, training, and correction. Inappropriate responses include out-of-control anger, ridicule or avoidance (no response).

3. Are you openly discussing spiritual growth issues within your family?

We don't need to be biblical scholars to know that God loves us and to sense the leading of the Spirit. But we do need to be willing to actively learn and grow in understanding of the gospel, and to share what we learn with our spouse and our children and other people.

4. Is your family involved in a community that shares your faith and values?

We can best help our sons and daughters make wise choices when we share a support system for living in a way that honors God.

5. Are you attentive to your own health as well as the health of family members?

6
Father Son Camaraderie

Sons disappoint their fathers, and fathers disappoint their sons. They both have high expectations of each other. A good relationship between them requires that expectations be tempered by love, and it also requires the readiness to forgive one another for wrongdoings.

Love and forgiveness are found at the center of healthy and strong father-son relationships. They are more important than a son's respect for his dad's authority or the father's provision of a stable home base for his son (although these things also rank high on God's list of priorities for us). Boys yearn for the love of their father. As they get older, they value his heart (if dad is present) because a male mentor is needed to shepherd them into the world of men.

It's easy for fathers to miss the opportunity of bringing their sons to a healthy understanding of manhood. Fathers may sometimes be absent because of an out-of-balance work life, and they simply do not prioritize the time to actively take part in their son's experience of growing up. Or they may diminish their role because, in one way or another, they embrace the expectation of a "generation gap," the generally accepted notion that older and younger people can not understand each other.

Don't Embrace the Generation Gap

As an expectation regarding relationships between fathers and sons, the generation gap can become a self-fulfilling prophecy. It may also serve as an excuse for fathers to drop the ball regarding spiritual matters.

Far too many of us dads are more involved in our son's three-point shot, fastball throw, or soccer skills than in his development as a godly man. On the other hand, experience has shown that if we invest even just a few hours each month in the process of discussing spiritual growth with our sons, each of us becomes a better man.

It is also important for fathers to recognize that *GOD HAS NO GRANDCHILDREN* - we are given the privilege of bringing our sons and daughters to a saving knowledge of Jesus so that they can choose to become adopted into the family of God. As temporary stewards of His children, we look to God's Word to learn what He wants for us and from us as fathers. We observe our sons to discover how God has made them, to identify their character traits, interests, abilities, strengths and weaknesses.

We do not impose our own character traits, interests, abilities, and weaknesses on our sons. Nor do we force them to enjoy what we enjoy. Instead, we encourage, teach, and direct them. We assist them in setting boundaries on their activities so that they can live in a way that is pleasing to God.

And we tell them stories about things that are real, not tall tales or overstatements of our accomplishments. Our kids eventually see through such falsehoods and exaggerations as a lack of truthfulness.

When we tell the truth about significant events and lessons in our life and those accounts stand up in real life, then our children learn and benefit from our experiences. Such genuineness is particularly important when we address spiritual topics, when we speak about matters of the heart and soul.

> These commandments
> that I give you today
> are to be upon your hearts.
> Impress them on your children.
> Talk about them when you sit at home
> and when you walk along the road,
> when you lie down
> and when you get up.
> — Deuteronomy 6:6-7

Sometimes the world stands still for a moment, and we consider the future of our sons.... What challenges will they face? What choices will they make? What kind of men will they become?

We don't really know what will happen to our children during their time on this earth. We don't even have that much control over tomorrow. So what is a father to do? Worry? Well, that's certainly in our nature, but it is not a father's calling.

Coming Alongside Your Son

There are many ways a father can care for his son. We should be, for instance, responsible providers, role models, and faithful husbands. However, I believe that the most precious gift a father can give his son is to be his spiritual mentor, combining unconditional love and discipline with biblical counsel. And the heart of that solid biblical counsel is to, at all costs, find life's meaning by knowing the God who made you. Both fathers and sons need to seek wisdom from God's Word, hold on to its instruction, put it in their hearts, make it their top priority, and act according to it.

> **Wisdom is supreme;**
> **therefore get wisdom.**
> Though it cost all you have,
> get understanding.
> — Proverbs 4: 7

Without vision and without a mentor, foolish boys may grow up to be foolish men, and at times they end up harming themselves and the people around them. Although the path to becoming a godly man is a narrow one, we can assure our sons that the journey is worth traveling. As men who are further along that path, we know that testing will come—as it does with any worthwhile undertaking in life. Yet we also can attest to the fact that many men, by God's grace, break free of their own self interests and walk the path of spiritual growth successfully.

In Hebrews 12 and 13, the Christian life is compared to a long-distance race. In the terms of this metaphor, we fathers are to come alongside our sons as they enter that race and then coach them along the way. We can jog with them side by side from time to time and show them how to read the trail signs. We can encourage them to make choices that bring them closer to God so that they will continue to move ahead in the right direction. We can help them to endure difficult times by reminding them that God is their spiritual father who loves them, knows what is best, and gives them strength and courage. We can encourage them to listen to God and respond to His directives when they sense His active influence in their thoughts and actions. In addition we can challenge them to stay connected with other men who are walking with God.

Along the way to becoming a godly man, our son will make mistakes and stumble. One of the many lessons we can teach our son is that *FAILURE IS NOT FINAL*. Because of God's enduring love and demonstration of that love through His son, we look to our future with hope. That's why learning from older men who are still "in process" is an important—and healthy—part of growing up.

Guidance from Above and Within

Another central truth of Christianity is that GOD SPEAKS TO US. Although many fathers can relate to the concept of God communicating to us through His written Word, reading the Bible is not the only way that we hear the voice of God. It is certainly important that we read and meditate on the scriptures and share what we learn with our children in order to enhance their understanding of God. However, as Christians, we are also indwelled and actively influenced by the Holy Spirit.

The Spirit enriches our understanding and application of God's Word to our lives, and enables us to know God better than we could have experienced even if Jesus was walking the earth during our lifetime. The amazing result is voice recognition: we learn to actually recognize those moments when God is speaking to us.

> When he has brought out all his own,
> he goes on ahead of them,
> and his sheep follow him
> because **they know his voice**.
> — John 10:4

The development of spiritual maturity comes from a relationship with God that involves daily decisions on our part to yield to His influence. He has given us the freedom to either live selfishly or to allow Jesus Christ to draw us out of our self-centeredness. This way of life can be defined, exemplified, and cultivated by fathers: the older Christian generation can nurture the next generation spiritually. When this doesn't happen, God still has his ways of drawing our children to Him through the example and leadership of others. But when we take the time and effort to point the way, families and communities benefit greatly and the deepest and most fulfilling relationship between father and son has the chance to develop.

Breaking from the "Drop Off" Culture

It's easy to become entangled in auto "drop off" activities, shuttling our kids from one program to another, dropping them off and picking them up so frequently that our cars become the focus of our life together as a family. **How do we slow down, at least occasionally, and spend time with our kids and other families in a way that fosters great communication about the important things in life?** At our church we found at least one answer to that question: by gathering together in intergenerational groups that focus on spiritual growth. With the encouragement of our spouses, several dads started a father-son fellowship group, where dads stay with their sons instead of dropping them off. Over time we realized that our boys and young men who were mentored in this way remained committed to an active faith walk through the college years and beyond.

Pizza and a Hike

The pizza parlor in Idyllwild, California, is like many small-town gathering spots with its jukebox music, video games, and bench seating at family-sized tables. Because Idyllwild is a mountain community, there was a chill in the air that Friday evening.

I sipped on a soda with one other dad, and our twelve-year-old sons drifted about the restaurant, moving from a video game... to just outside the entry door... and then hopping on the bench with questions for us. "Who are we waiting for?" We're not sure who's coming, but we expect a few friends. "How far is the cabin?" We could walk there from here. "How high will we hike tomorrow?" Three thousand feet up from here if we make it to the top.

I had as many questions as the boys did—if not more. After all, the start of a new ministry is filled with unknowns. Every one of the entering-sixth-grade boys and their dads in our church had been invited to share this weekend adventure in Idyllwild. The purpose was to establish a network of fathers and sons who would meet together regularly to discuss spiritual things. Letters and e-mails were sent and phone calls were made, but attendance at this event didn't look promising. Sports, hobbies, recreational activities, and other family commitments were scheduled for the same weekend. The typical response had been a less-than-encouraging "Maybe." OK, if you do come, meet me at the pizza parlor in the center of Idyllwild.

Although I guarded my expectations, I also prepared for the weekend. In the preceding weeks, I had found a suitable trail to explore with our sons, worked up some Bible lessons that we dads could share with the boys during the hike, reproduced a dozen photocopies of the lessons, and put together a possible agenda of topics for meetings throughout the coming year. I had done all of these things prayerfully, and God's Spirit seemed to be moving the process along. A core group of four dads (who had been connected by four visionary moms) seemed to be committed to this idea, but we had much to discuss if this group were to become a reality. Would there be enough dads attending this adventure-and-planning weekend to make the effort of establishing a new ministry worthwhile? That matter was in God's hands.

As I sat in the pizza parlor, praying for God to bring who he would to this gathering, another dad and his son arrived. Three fathers and three sons – that works for me, time to order the pizza— but wait! Two more fathers and their sons are at the door. Wow! "Great to see you here." Then the restaurant door opened again. Another father-son pair! More greetings… followed by the arrival of two other father-son pairs. Bring on the pizza!

For me, this was the first of several "God things"—those happenings that our Lord seems to orchestrate—that occurred during our weekend together. Another one, for example, was that some of the arriving fathers and sons were dealing with mild sickness, and the planned hike was strenuous. Nevertheless, all eight fathers and eight sons hiked the next day, periodically stopping along the trail so that we dads could share Bible lessons with our sons. The sick members of our group dropped off at various points. "See you on the way down," they said. About half the group proceeded to the summit, and there enjoyed a time of prayer and rest. Somehow, pair by pair, those fathers and sons who were battling illness unexpectedly joined us at the top as well.

When we started back down the mountain, this group of fathers and sons were walking together on much more than a hike. We had begun an interconnected spiritual journey that, for many of us, continues to this day.

When will you be ordering the first pizza for your group? A father who struggles with passing on his faith based upon his own efforts can augment the development of his son's spiritual life through his connections with other dads. We have observed that the contributions of fathers to their son's faith and maturity are enriched in father-son networks that tackle serious issues.

Raising Expectations

Consider for a moment how healthy churches equip dads for their role as their family's spiritual leader. The church often encourages parents to be the primary teachers of their children and promotes a solid partnership between the church and the home in the effort to raise children in the knowledge of God. It may also provide home devotional resources and encourage men to be involved in support groups. Fellowship activities may be organized, perhaps including a weekly men's Bible study and an annual men's retreat. Fathers are encouraged to teach Sunday school and are challenged to be involved in the youth programs.

Although this typical approach does result in spiritual growth for men and boys, it doesn't tap into the full potential of dads gathering to mentor their sons. Father-son groups enable older men to know and sometimes influence their son's peers. Boys and young men also come to know and be mentored by more than one older man.

Father-son groups that focus on spiritual growth are rare these days, but imagine young boys being aware that their adolescent years would include special times with dad, perhaps within the context of their local church. Imagine these boys having the opportunity to get to know other godly men who would both model and foster their spiritual growth. These boys would know that, in addition to their own dad, they would have a body of men encouraging them and praying for them (this becomes particularly important for boys being raised by single moms). These boys would also look forward to participating in unique ceremonies of affirmation at key points along the way (more about this in Appendix A).

Now imagine fathers looking forward to their son's teen years when they—together with other dads—would have the opportunity to really know his peer group; to actively pray with their son and his Christian peers; and to follow a plan for intentionally guiding their son to spiritual maturity (while the dads themselves also grow in the process).

Instead of getting a potentially isolated or biased viewpoint from their father alone, sons hear several fathers sharing candidly about the topic at hand. Likewise, fathers see the responses of many sons—who are sometimes more willing to speak because they are safely surrounded by their peers. The group leader brings the different viewpoints into alignment with one another and especially with God's Word by using sound biblical resources (available at www.fathersons.org).

The media's role models of men depict self-centered fools; long gone are the days of *Father Knows Best*. If this type of father-son ministry is to succeed, men must take on the leadership roles and, relying on the power of the Holy Spirit, direct the meetings, moderate the social events, and make the service projects happen. Practical suggestions are provided in Appendices A and B of this book.

And When He Becomes An Adult...

Fortunately dads have a choice: we can decide to live as real men who are growing in our knowledge of God, our love for Him, and walk with Him, and we can band together with other fathers to pass this vision of manhood to our sons. I am so thankful to the men and women who encouraged me to not attempt fatherhood alone. I needed God and other dads for support, and my son Michael needed to have relationships with mentors other than me as well as boys who were on the right path, especially during the tumultuous teen years.

Now that my son has graduated from college, I appreciate even more the process Michael and I and our band of fathers and sons have been through. I am learning about the changing relationship between a father and his adult son. Michael has moved from our home and is becoming financially independent despite a difficult economy. But Michael is not alone, and he knows that his success in life is not entirely dependent on his own strength. Because of his own relationship to God, he has a good foundation and he will certainly be a blessing to others. For me, his passage into adulthood is less like "passing the torch" and more like "passing the paddle."

Breaking Through

It can be difficult to judge the pattern of inbound waves along the California coastline on a windy morning in early spring. But my son and I were up for an adventure together - we had carried the kayaks to the sand and we intended to get through that surf in order to paddle on to our destination a few miles northward along the coast.

Large pelicans were cruising by, confidently drifting over the waves with their 5 foot wingspans, as if to say "it's easy." We could also see the seals jumping off the rock formations some distance offshore, swimming through the whitecaps with ease. Moderately warm air, cold water, clouds drifting by - time to jump in.

What is it about us men that we become so alive when we leave our comfort zones and dive into something that challenges us physically? In addition to the health benefits of activities that get us moving, men need to take risks (occasionally and within reason) as part of our pathway to maturity. And us older guys need to introduce younger men to the many healthy ways to get out, get active, face the uncertainties of nature - learning more about ourselves and the world around us in the process. For Michael and me, the activities in nature have included surfing, mountain hiking, white water rafting, and ocean kayaking.

"OK dad, let's go". Today Michael had chosen to lead the way, so he grabbed the paddle with one hand and pulled the kayak with the other as he ran into the water. A large wave suddenly formed, and I was tempted to shout a warning. Fortunately another instinct - respect for a man's effort - kept me silent as I watched Michael jump into the kayak and paddle straight at the wave.

Michael may or may not have misjudged his entry timing, but he knew what to do with the situation as it unfolded. Any hesitation would have resulted in a hard tumble (it had happened to both of us before), but his fast and straight approach resulted in a thrilling cut through the wave as it crashed toward the shore. Maneuvering just beyond the break zone, my adult son looked back at me as if to say "don't worry dad, I'm watching out for you."

My attention returned to the rhythm of incoming waves, and then I made my dash. I did not judge my own entry well and was almost drenched during the resulting battle with the waves, but soon father and son were paddling into the open ocean. This particular outing required us to overcome additional waves as we stopped to explore a beach along the coast, and at one point we enjoyed a close encounter with several dolphins. We eventually returned to our starting point having pushed ourselves to experience nature together.

My own father will be 90 years old soon. His ability to challenge nature with such outings has been set aside. My siblings and I now help him with basic tasks, and we are aware of our role during his final years. "Don't worry dad, we're watching out for you."

Love, respect, faith, hope - these things can be shared from one generation to another. We can break through many barriers if we are willing to make the effort, face our fears, and take risks as only men can do when they work and play together while also taking time to address the meaningful things in life.

When you experience the joy of helping someone, or discover inexplicable peace amid chaos... When you have the presence of mind to respond to anger with kindness; or rally the strength to resist evil... When you find the gift of gentle words that can encourage someone who is hurting... Moments like these are evidence of a Spirit-guided transformation occurring within us. God is at work, and you are becoming genuine... A real man.

When You're Ready, Son

When your impulses say, "Let's go" and excitement is calling
Yet you pause to discern right from wrong, good from bad…

When the promise you made becomes sour obligation
Yet you rally your strength to finish the task…

When temptation puts before you a sensual lure
Yet you look away and focus on a better vision of love…

When you fail or face rejection, get sick or become injured
Yet find peace in God's presence for the journey ahead…

When you make a wrong choice and suffer the consequences
Yet admit fault and grow stronger as you continue to learn…

When family or friends, neighbors or co-workers are unkind
Yet you continue to build up and care for those around you…

When you fear that things are out of control
Yet you trust in God's goodness and step into tomorrow…

Then be assured, my son, that you are ready
For the brotherhood of godly men
*Who reach out each day for others to join us
On a spiritual journey rich in meaning and love…
Who, like you and me, don't deserve
to be part of this fellowship*
Yet we're accepted, just as we are, by our Father above.

Questions for Contemplation Or Discussion...

1. How well do you know your son?

Perhaps it is time for a fresh appraisal of his character traits, interests, abilities, strengths and weaknesses.

2. How well do you know your son's friends?

It is well worth the effort for you and your spouse to take a look at the people your son is spending time with. Getting to know his acquaintances and their parents can open your eyes to potential new family friends, or you may discover issues you need to address.

3. Are there men of God in your circle of relationships that would be willing to really get to know your son?

In our society today, men rarely gather to intentionally discuss important life issues, much less to consider deep spiritual questions involving the purpose of our existence and other matters of the soul. That reality has serious consequences for adults, but I think the consequences are even more serious for our sons.

4. Are you willing to consider meeting with other fathers and sons to share the journey of faith with them?

It may be time for you to take the initiative and form a small group of fathers and sons that meet together occasionally to discuss spiritual matters. In addition, boys in fatherless homes need to be touched by older men who will take initiative and mentor them.

7
Let's Get Real

Having explored what it means to be a real man (chapter 1) and how such men relate to God (chapter 2), to each other (chapter 3), to women and, Lord willing, to one spouse (chapter 4), and to the next generation (chapters 5 and 6), we're ready to better understand the process of spiritual transformation that enables Christians to love sincerely and occasionally rise above the self absorbed world we live in. Although men live in the world and certainly appreciate the beauty and complexity of its design, we know that what is "natural' is not always good. In fact, we need to question our own desires and motivations because the propensity for depravity is embedded in ourselves - intertwined with our ability to exhibit noble character and righteousness.

Many believers underestimate the necessity of a fundamental change regarding their approach to daily life. We can deal with deep issues of growth only if we are willing to (1) recognize our shortcomings, (2) acknowledge our inability to solve them on our own, and (3) actively respond to a new relationship with God. On an ongoing basis, this includes honestly addressing issues of our heart which the indwelling Spirit reveals to us.

Although they sometimes see themselves as free men, those who try to go it alone and who deal with life's core issues using their own power inevitably end up in bondage to their sinful nature. Those who allow Jesus Christ to fundamentally change them become men who are free to recognize and resist evil, and who are able to make good choices. However, godly men don't always perform up to their potential.

When we speak of athletic men, intelligent men, powerful men, and gifted men, we know that these men are not perfect in their athleticism, intelligence, power, or giftedness—and we do not expect perfection. Men of God are also human beings who fail to be godly at times—and, only too aware of their limitations, they aren't all that surprised when they do. Godly men know they are far from perfect.

Nobody's Perfect

When we label a man as an athlete, we mean that he is stronger, more talented, and more skilled than most of us and that most of the time his performance reflects that reality. But we are not surprised when he makes a mistake or falls short of expectations from time to time—when he gets a double bogey, misses the fly ball, fouls out of the basketball game, or fumbles the football.

Mature Christian men are obviously not virtuous every moment of every day. They get distracted from their focus on God, miss an opportunity to love as he would have them love, lose their temper and foul out in a relationship, and fumble in their efforts to serve with humility. In fact, the godliest men I know are very aware of their own faults and shortcomings, and they have no trouble calling their sin, sin. But they don't give up on themselves because they don't give up on God. They return to Him and pursue excellence because they know that He will strengthen them to do the right thing at just the right time.

> Do you not know? Have you not heard?
> The LORD is the everlasting God,
> the Creator of the ends of the earth.
> He will not grow tired or weary,
> and his understanding no one can fathom.
> He gives strength to the weary and increases the power of the weak.
> **Even youths grow tired and weary,**
> **and young men stumble and fall;**
> **but those who hope in the LORD will renew their strength.**
> They will soar on wings like eagles;
> they will run and not grow weary,
> they will walk and not be faint.
> — Isaiah 40:28-31

Of course this raises an important question: How do we figure out what God wants each of us to do? I believe we learn about how God wired us and what he wants from us by an appropriate mix of devotion (letting go of self-centered ambitions and desires and letting God direct us) and activity (doing things in response to our best understanding of God's leading each day).

However, some men do not want to address the topic of faith and spiritual growth because they have accepted the misconception that their life will be unhappy if they really commit themselves to God. Others of us, aware of our limitations, may be uncomfortable about our spiritual life because we put "spiritual people" on a pedestal; we may not feel qualified to even talk about faith issues.

A significant part of growing up is acknowledging and gaining an understanding of the spiritual dimension of life rather than choosing to ignore it. As we reflect on the crashing ocean waves or an awe-inspiring mountain range; as we experience the heights of love or wrestle with the consequences of hatred; as we attempt to understand depression or appreciate the exhilaration of true joy, we realize there is much more to life than the physical stuff. Something else is going on, and that "something else" is the spiritual dimension of life, the dimension we explore together as we read God's Word and learn to walk in his Spirit.

A Difference from Within

As Christians, you and I are called to be transformed in the way that we think about things. That kind of change is not easy for us men. To begin with, many of us are "doers" instead of "thinkers," and so it is difficult for us to enter into the self examination process that is part of changing the way we choose one course of action over another. It's easy for us to get wrapped up in the pace of daily activities and to leave God outside of our thoughts.

The world's ways are indeed enticing. We are bombarded with the allure of bigger homes, faster cars, enhanced sex, sumptuous food, higher incomes, better clothes, and superior sports equipment.

Advertising techniques cultivate our desire for these things. The problem is that these things can never bring true happiness. As we chase after them, we learn that the satisfaction they offer is temporary at best. Our basic problem can never be solved by things in the world, because it is an issue inside of us.

Our pursuit of pleasure will never result in contentment because we will always want more than the next man and more than we currently have. This desire for more can't be solved unless we shift our focus. We overcome this issue by focusing less on ourselves and more on God.

> **Do not conform any longer**
> **to the pattern of this world,**
> **but be transformed**
> **by the renewing of your mind.**
> Then you will be able to test
> and approve what God's will is—
> his good, pleasing and perfect will.
> — Romans 12:2

In our inner being—in our heart and mind—we fight a battle of good versus evil. We are therefore wise to willingly question our natural responses, prayerfully consider whether our choices are right, and, if we sense that something is wrong with an activity or the people involved, boldly refrain from going along with the crowd. Godly men become increasingly aware of moral issues that many of those around them are either incapable of perceiving or unwilling to address.

> When a man is getting better
> he understands more and more clearly the evil that is still in him.
> When a man is getting worse
> he understands his own badness less and less…
> This is common sense, really.
> **You understand sleep when you are awake,**
> **not while you are sleeping**…
> You can understand the nature of drunkenness
> when you are sober, not when you are drunk..

> **Good people know about both good and evil:
> bad people do not know about either**.
> — C. S. Lewis, *Mere Christianity*

Although we are not naturally drawn to do the right things at all times, we can make good decisions more often if we understand our propensity for evil and if we evaluate our options based upon a sincere desire to walk closely with God. And our Lord knows how sincere that desire is. In fact, He—who is primarily interested in the genuine growth of our character into Christ likeness—looks right past our actions, good or bad, and weighs the motives of our heart.

We face opposition of various kinds as we grow in faith, and our ability to recognize evil improves with our increased awareness of spiritual things. I saw the impact of evil in a new way once I became a father, because decadent behaviors are now represented by pop culture as though they are normal lifestyles. Immoral acts are endorsed in the name of tolerance, and this situation highlights the need for Christian fathers to articulate to their children what the Word of God says about errant values embraced by our society. One positive outcome of these "in your face" conflicts between right and wrong is that families are forced to deal with spiritual matters, if they take the time to discuss important issues and honestly pursue the truth.

Honesty and Integrity

The engineer uses the word *integrity* to describe something that is true to its design, something that serves its purpose, something that is safe and reliable. Integrity—in buildings and in human beings—must be tested in good times and bad times to determine if it is real.

Integrity in a man is the quality of possessing and steadfastly adhering to what is true and genuine, even when doing so is difficult and especially when we face opposition. It is what we become when we live congruent with our authentic self, rooted in Christ. In a recent personal email message to me regarding Ephesians 6:10-17, my friend Steve Olsen described how honesty and truthfulness are strongly related to how men of God prepare to take a stand against spiritual forces of evil:

> In order for real men to "be strong in the Lord"
> and "stand firm against the schemes of the devil"
> the FIRST thing they need to do
> is to prepare themselves with "non-concealment" –
> the etymological root of the Greek word "aletheia" or "truth."
> It's not "God's truth" (that's the sword of the Spirit that comes later),
> instead it's wrapping ourselves in integrity, honesty,
> no masks, what you see is what you get,
> truth in the sense of being true to that which really is there,
> faithfully representing what is,
> "high fidelity" people, i.e., "true".
> This belt of truth is not a piece of armor
> but the key first preparatory thing we need to do
> if we are going to be successful in the battles of the day
> and in defeat of the father of lies and deception,
> who works hard to get us to live in something
> other than reality and truth,
> (e.g., think of ourselves as better than we are,
> present a "better" image to others).
> In contrast, we need to be men who are honest
> and transparent about whom we really are
> with ourselves, with others and with God.
> Not a normal thing in our world or even in our Christian circles.
> No wonder we never get out of the starting gate....
> — Steve Olsen, 11.26.2010

Instead of being transparent, we often tell lies to conceal who we really are. We may want to evade the consequences of our actions, to avoid doing something we don't want to do, to not hurt someone's feelings, or just to make ourselves look good. Whatever the venue—whether academics, sports, or business—we also cheat to get more than we have earned. Will we be appreciated and loved if people see who we really are, with all of our imperfections? We are often afraid to face the consequences of being genuine, being ourselves... being a real man.

I like the term "real man" because it gets to the heart of integrity. It challenges us to become genuine, rather than fake. Jesus does not ask men to be something they are not. Instead, He says "learn from me, for I am gentle and humble in heart, and you will find rest for your souls." (Matthew 18:29) Any man in relationship with Jesus becomes a man who is secure in who he is, with all his shortcomings, because he knows that he is appreciated and loved by God Himself.

> The man of integrity walks securely,
> but he who takes crooked paths will be found out.
> — Proverbs 10:9

Sometimes we tell "white lies" because we don't want to hurt a person's feelings. We might, for instance, say, "You did a great job" when in fact that person has not performed very well. It is usually possible, however, to be positive without lying. The comments "I can really see improvement" (if you can) and "I'm proud of you" (if you are) are more appropriate and honest responses. After all, people really do appreciate truth more than flattery—and we should be loving and tactful when we speak the truth to them. The truth that we speak stands the test of time, in contrast to lies that will eventually be exposed.

> He who rebukes a man
> will in the end gain more favor
> than he who has a flattering tongue.
> — Proverbs 28:23

Each day brings choices for us to make: When to awake, how to greet our spouse or children, what to eat, who to listen to, what to read, where to go, what to wear... The choices we make reveal who we really are. Do they reflect a desire to please ourselves, or do they point toward higher motives? Do they reflect a sincere love of God and others?

God's love can only be fully understood in light of what He has revealed about Himself in the Bible, which focuses on Jesus - the

Word that became flesh (John 1:1-5), the one and only Son of God (John 3:16), the image of the invisible God (Colossians 1:15), the radiance of God's glory and representation of His being (Hebrews 1:3). Therefore Jesus enables us to truly know God, and to live true to our design as adopted members of His family.

Not the Typical Picture of a Real Man

Having scratched the surface of what it means to grow up in Christ, let's return to the basic issue of casting a vision of what it means to grow up and become a real man. Many boys and men have been inspired by Rudyard Kipling's poem "If" ("If you can keep your head when all about you are losing theirs and blaming it on you..."), William Henley's poem "Invictus" ("I am the master of my fate: I am the captain of my soul…"), and the writings of Alfred Tennyson (including "The Charge of the Light Brigade"). These authors and many others portray the real man as one who acts on his convictions, rebounds from defeat, takes risks, remains on task despite adversity, and embraces high moral values. Men who overcame impossible odds capture our imagination and inspire us to stand tall and "do what it takes."

I love stories of great men and heroes, but I have also asked the following question in the course of writing this book: How would Jesus describe a real man? After studying His words as recorded in the four gospels, one thing is clear: Jesus challenges our views of success and He generally asks men to evaluate their own attitudes and motives and avoid comparing themselves to others. He upholds men and women who are not considered by the world to be heroes. Instead His focus is on those who admit their shortcomings and who acknowledge their dependence on God. He raises a standard of being "all in" in terms of our personal loyalty to God – a state of mind that frees us to become the real men that God has designed us to be.

Jesus was not easily impressed with the accomplishments of men. He always looked to the heart of people He interacted with, expressing appreciation of actions that flow from a sincere faith while openly criticizing other self serving attempts to earn favor with God and men. As if to say "it's what's inside a man that counts," while at the same time recognizing that a man's actions flow from what's inside - hence everything about us men counts.

I suppose we could paint a picture of real men as an unworthy group of guys who find the wisdom and power to grow spiritually as they come to understand that they are adopted sons of God. As we read and contemplate the Word of God, and as we respond to the leading of His spirit, our viewpoint is expanded; God gets bigger and we get smaller, and His love changes us.

Our view of God and our understanding of His love need to be challenged and refreshed. And there is no better joy in life for us fathers than genuine relationships with our own children as well as other children (particularly from fatherless homes) that have been forged over time, that include an ever-widening circle of love, and that result in entire families deciding together to walk with God.

Serving with Dad

The night air was cool and still, a welcome refreshment and sharp contrast to the hot, sweaty, dirty, noisy work of the day. Brilliant stars filled the sky above the group of sixth-grade boys who, thankfully, did not have a close encounter with a Catalina Island rattlesnake while they were chopping down thistle bushes. And the boys had a good laugh at the idea of shipping a case of RoundUp to the camp so they wouldn't have to wrestle with the same bushes next year.

Now, though, the boys were quieter, aware of the dark expanse of ocean between them and home, seeing the orange glow of light coming from the California shoreline, and listening to one of the dads talk about the truth that Christian men serve God by serving others. With external distractions at a minimum, the boys were able to listen closely.

Having spent the day as they had, the boys were able to really hear the message. After all, they had found some joy in serving. They'd experienced a special bond and partnership with one another as they worked harder together than any of them do at home. And, although they wouldn't have worded it this way, they had tasted the contentment that comes with being where God wants you to be and doing what He wants you to do. So the teacher's words rang true in a different way than they would have a month ago at a father-son meeting on the mainland.

The evening closed with prayer. The dads' prayers were honest and open. The tired boys' prayers were somewhat rote but still heartfelt. It had been a good day, one in which God was clearly at work growing these young men into strong men of God.

It takes a special ministry to welcome fifteen fathers and their sixth-grade sons to work at its retreat center, but InterVarsity's Campus by the Sea on Catalina Island has welcomed our FAST groups year after year. And each time the Memorial Day weekend of working and playing and service and fun becomes an amazing experience for fathers and sons alike.

One dad commented, "I've never seen my son work this hard!" And the work is hard. Through the years, the boys have cleared brush, moved large rocks from one end of the beach to the other, scrubbed the dining-hall patio deck, and prepared the cabins for summertime visitors by cleaning the bathrooms, scrubbing down the cabins, and removing the plywood sheets that cover the window openings (there's no glass!) and protect the cabins during the winter rains.

The boys start asking during the winter if the FAST group is going to Catalina again this year. And early on the boys start planning who's going to do the dishes - the kitchen's commercial dishwashing hose and sprayer is a real crowd pleaser!

The dads pray and plan for the teaching and worship times, and it's always gratifying to hear the boys talk about those teachings at breakfast the next morning, during the day as they work, and even throughout the next year. This year the boys themselves will be playing guitar and leading the worship times. (Hearing the voices of dads and their boys singing praise to God really does give you hope for the future!)

The opportunity to serve at Campus by the Sea has taught the boys that serving the Lord may at times be hard, but it's often enjoyable and always rewarding. Yes, Christian men serve—and we are blessed when we do.

Spiritual maturity demands that we prioritize people over things. It requires that we listen more than talk, that we encourage (give hope, confidence, and courage) rather than criticize, and that we forgive rather than blame. Many things in this world and in our own sin nature get in the way of this type of fellowship. Fear, pride, resentment, vengeance, cruelty, and injustice are just some of those hindrances. God, however, enables us, by the power of the Holy Spirit, to live a life characterized by the practice of being sincerely sympathetic and compassionate toward people.

> Now that you have purified yourselves
> by obeying the truth
> so that you have sincere love for your brothers,
> **love one another deeply,**
> **from the heart**.
> — 1 Peter 1:22

Kindness

God's view of kindness is broad and far reaching. It involves everything from small actions on our part...to lifestyle changes...to major decisions we make. But kindness begins with simply caring about people. Even in the business world, this quality is recognized as a vital part of effective leadership. U.S. business leader Jack Welch described successful leaders this way: "People with passion care—really care to the bones—about colleagues, employees, and friends winning. They love to learn and grow, and they get a huge kick when the people around them do the same."

When life is going well for us, we find it relatively easy to be content and hopeful and to love God and the people around us. But challenging times—seasons of sickness, disappointment, failure, mistreatment by others, natural disasters, accidents—rock our world and test our character (read more about this in Appendix D of this book). Even when the circumstances of life are tough and painful, relentless and, from a human perspective, hopeless, God calls us to keep on loving Him and the people around us.

How do we avoid obsessing over tribulations, and continue to love others in the midst of our own difficulties? As with so many aspects of the Christian life, the answers to this question include our mind-set or mental outlook. We need to choose to focus on the truth that God never abandons us and that He wants the very best for us. He is always in control and knows all about our suffering. God provides the strength we need; He guides our steps; and He walks alongside us. Our part is to keep focused on Him.

> Consider it pure joy, my brothers,
> whenever you face trials of many kinds,
> because you know that the testing
> of your faith develops perseverance.
> Perseverance must finish its work
> so that you may be mature and complete,
> not lacking anything.
> — James 1:2-4

Perseverance and Hope

Study the art, calendars, and inventions of ancient people, and you learn that those who came thousands of years before us were not any less intelligent than we are. Certainly we have access to an accumulation of scientific knowledge that was unavailable to them, but their accomplishments and wisdom are worthy of our attention.

In fact, it is possible that the ancients were able to hear the voice of God more clearly and easily in part because their life had less noise and commotion. People living hundreds of years ago were not exposed to the bombardment of electronic input that fills our life today. It is no surprise to me that they were able to see, in Job's words, "the destiny of all who forget God" (Job 8:12). As both he and, two thousand years later, Shakespeare observed, there is no hope without God (*Macbeth*, Act V Scene V).

Many of the intellectual giants of science and philosophy who do not know God have concluded that life on this earth is meaningless (a perspective also recognized as the "ontologically fatal insight"). Without hope for eternal life beyond our years on earth, without faith in any purposeful, personal, and loving being more powerful than humankind, people are reduced to shadows. And even worse is the state of men who have become slaves to superstitions and other irrational belief systems.

A biblical view of our eternal future impacts the way we live each day in the present, whatever challenges we face, because the big issue of life has been settled. Those of us who believe in the saving work of Jesus Christ know that the destiny of our soul is both certain and glorious. Having chosen to accept the salvation God offers us, we have become part of His family, and we look forward to being at home with Him.

> Do not let your hearts be troubled.
> Trust in God; trust also in me.
> In my Father's house are many rooms;
> if it were not so, I would have told you.
> I am going there to prepare a place for you.

> And if I go and prepare a place for you,
> I will come back and take you to be with me
> that you also may be where I am.
> — John 14:1-3

The earth itself is destined for a remarkable change. The wild ride of future events (commonly referred to as the end times) which are described in the Bible are also difficult for us to put into sequence and connect with historic and current events. Many people have attempted to do so, but for two thousand years no one has been able to accurately put a timeline on God's program. Jesus Himself said that no one would know (Matthew 24:37, Acts 1:7).

It's exciting to anticipate the magnificence of living in a redeemed world with a restored body. Regardless of the corruption brought on by sin, I believe that this world occasionally gives us a hint of that heavenly glory. We may be able to imagine the joy of future heavenly activities as we appreciate music, sports, rest, travel, worship, moments of deep contentment, scenes of incredible beauty, or the experience of being loved. Indeed, earthly activities that stir your soul in a good way and are in line with God's will for you—those things just may be your foretaste of heaven, of your eternal destiny.

When we have our eternal destiny in mind, we can know courage rooted in the Lord, overcome our fears, and even enter into joy despite difficult circumstances. As with all good things in life, peace of mind is a gift from God.

> **Do not be anxious about anything**,
> but in everything, by prayer and petition,
> with thanksgiving, present your requests to God.
> And the peace of God,
> which transcends all understanding,
> will guard your hearts and your minds in Christ Jesus.
> — Philippians 4:6–7

Questions for Contemplation Or Discussion...

1. What does Jesus expect of mature, godly men?

By focusing less on ourselves and more on God, we come to a better understanding of reality. As we read and contemplate the Word of God, and as we respond to the leading of His spirit, our viewpoint is expanded; God gets bigger and we get smaller, and His love changes us. Ultimately we must rely upon God, not our own willpower, to bring about fundamental changes in each of us.

Then you will know the truth, and the truth will set you free...
So if the Son sets you free, you will be free indeed.
— John 8:32, 36

2. Why is it important to have a healthy understanding of our destiny?

Our view of the future impacts the way we live each day in the present, whatever challenges we face, because the big issue of life has been settled. Looking to life after death with God is the very essence of hope. Without hope for eternal life beyond our years on earth, without faith in any purposeful, personal, and loving being more powerful than humankind, people are reduced to shadows.

3. How do we stand our ground and keep our confidence during times of suffering?

As with so many aspects of the Christian life, the key seems to be our thoughts. We need to choose to focus on the truth that God never abandons us, that he wants the very best for us, that he is always in control, and that he knows all about our suffering. These truths are powerfully comforting and hope-filled.

Appendix A

Practical Ideas for Organizing a Father-Son Group

The central activity for a *Fathers And Sons Together*™ network is simple and yet profound: fathers and sons meet together in a host home or other facility on a bi-weekly or monthly basis to discuss spiritual matters—and to have fun doing it. The fellowship time at each session is:

> **Purpose-driven:** We're preparing our sons to be godly men and to appreciate the study and application of Scripture.
>
> **Interactive:** Fathers and sons share their own viewpoints, respond to questions, and give and receive advice.
>
> **Relevant to grade levels:** The discussions are appropriate to the sons' ages and current life experiences.
>
> **Grounded in prayer:** Leaders pray for the success of every meeting, and for good relationships between the older and younger men and boys. During each meeting, the fathers and sons are encouraged to pray out loud.

Over a decade of experience with many father-son groups at various churches have shown us that with diligent male leadership (and the support of wives and mothers), groups of four to twenty dads (at each grade level or sometimes overlapping several school grades) can and have stayed together for years. And we have learned many lessons along the way, including the following:

- Preparation for the teaching time is essential (the **www.fathersons.org** website and this book are outcomes of our own attempts to develop leadership resources).

- Dads and sons need to have significant time together in situations that foster their getting to know one another. We have learned that each session is precious: expect God to bless the time you and your son spend honoring Him together.

- Fun times are important for just about every gathering. Begin and end the discussion times with fun activity.

- Don't miss the opportunity to talk about current topics that matter. Discuss the ways that spiritual things impact our everyday lives as men.

- Don't be discouraged by the constant battle to find a meeting time that works. Scheduling has always been a major challenge for father-son groups. Let me reassure you that every time you get frustrated with the obstacles that pop up, God will do something unexpected and then you'll be rolling again.

You may be asking yourself, "Do the dads who teach need to be biblical scholars?" No! Father-son groups welcome dads with widely different backgrounds, skills, spiritual gifts, and levels of scriptural knowledge—and the Lord uses all of us. The group leader should be well grounded in the Word, but he doesn't need a Bible college diploma or a seminary degree.

The only requirement for each participating dad is a heart for God and the desire to see that their son walk the path in life that God outlines in his Word. In fact, a dad with limited biblical knowledge can still inspire family by studying God's Word with his son, encouraging his son to learn more, and discussing with him what both of them are learning. Father-son groups are a great place for dads as well as sons to grow in their faith.

Overcoming Obstacles

The major obstacle to starting up such a father-son group may not be what you would expect. We expected the boys to be hesitant. Would they even want to meet with us dads month after month, year after year? Would they want to talk about spiritual things? To our surprise, their answer to these questions was a resounding yes.

Unexpectedly, the difficulty most groups have encountered has almost always been with the dads; it seems that kids often want relationship while dads are somewhat afraid of it. And then there is the difficulty of finding men willing to be leaders. Our original group was able to leverage a network of families of sixth-grade boys that had already been established by some of our wives. Other groups have been set up with the assistance of church staff members.

An additional challenge was convincing dads to make the father-son group a priority in their busy schedules. After much prayer, many dads have done exactly that, and the rewards are priceless. The combination of dads with other dads, dads with one another's sons, and sons with their peers—all at the same time—yields unexpected benefits and blessings. As one dad said, "Our boys want to be there. And it's awesome to see men bonding together to help their sons know Christ and struggling together through the difficult issues of life."

Addressing Age Appropriate Issues

In the years before their son enters the sixth grade, dads are encouraged to lay the groundwork for future initiation into the world of men. That foundational work includes praying for their son's spiritual growth, explaining basic Christian doctrine, doing things with their son that get him into the outside world, reading stories together, discovering their son's unique interests and spiritual gifts, building their son's confidence based on his natural skills and his accomplishments, and connecting him with other Christian families.

We have found that the sixth-grade year is a key phase in father-son networks because of changes in the physical make up of the boys. During that time, the following activities are important:

- Attend a series of father-son meetings where moral values and Christian beliefs are discussed

- Have your son memorize a "life verse" – a bible verse that is special to him and that you help him discover

- Participate in a significant adventure with your son

- Memorize—with your son—the five principles for godly manhood

- Take part in an advancement ceremony and give your son a blessing

When their son is in seventh- and eighth- grade, fathers are encouraged to help him develop a heart open to the Lord, to deal with the new challenges he may face with the transition to middle school, to clearly address the physical and emotional changes of puberty, and to foster in him a genuine concern for others, an appreciation of public service, and a positive understanding of involvement in the church.

> **The combination of dads with other dads, dads with one another's sons, and sons with their peers—all at the same time—yields unexpected benefits and blessings.**

When the boys are in high school (ninth through twelfth grades), fathers are wise to maintain and reinforce their relationship with their son while clearly addressing the temptations of pornography and sexual promiscuity, fostering peer relationships of confession and prayer support, addressing deep questions of faith, preparing their son to defend his faith, and continuing to encourage their son on his path toward becoming a responsible adult. Our sons also participated in an advancement ceremony marking their high-school graduation.

Ceremonies, and a Father's Blessing

Ceremonies serve as a memorable way to both recognize the completion of one phase of a young man's life, and mark his passage into the next phase. At such a moment, a father's blessing is a significant gift. We see that at Jesus' baptism when his heavenly Father issued a public statement.

> As Jesus was coming up out of the water,
> he saw heaven being torn open
> and the Spirit descending on him like a dove.
> And a voice came from heaven:
> **"You are my Son, whom I love;**
> **with you I am well pleased."**
> — Mark 1:10-11

In his blessing, God included these three elements:

- ✓ "You are my Son,"
- ✓ "I love you," and
- ✓ "I am well pleased with you"
    —very significant words indeed.

At the father-son ceremony held at the end of sixth grade and marking the entrance into middle school, we have had the boys share their life verse and recite the five principals of authentic manhood they have memorized (see Appendix C). In addition, each dad gives his son a father's blessing.

Each father (or surrogate dad) compiles a list of the good qualities he has observed in his son. The following example is taken from the blessing I offered to my son Michael and the character traits I commented on:

(Son's name), I love you, and I am encouraged by the ways you are becoming a godly man.

You have many special qualities, and I want to mention a few of them.

1. *You have a good attitude about learning new things.*
2. *You have demonstrated a desire to spend time with friends who are a godly influence in your life.*
3. *You persevere in hard circumstances.*
4. *You have a sincere faith in God.*
5. *You are quick to say you're sorry.*
6. *You are coordinated, strong, fast, adventurous, and enthusiastic.*
7. *You communicate energetically.*

(Son's name), may God continue to bless you on your journey into manhood. Jesus will be with you each step of the way. Your mother and I will also help you as much as we can.

This ceremony has sometimes included the presentation of a sword, a symbol of God's Word (Ephesians 6:32). The gift of a sword to each son can add a lot of excitement to the ceremony—and a good amount of concern on the part of the moms! If real swords are presented, consider having them mounted for display in your son's room (for safety purposes).

At most major father-son commemorative events, we have found it appropriate for entire families to be present. A rather formal dinner is sometimes shared, and then the solemn ceremony occurs. At the high school graduation ceremonies, parents may present their son with a gift that uniquely celebrates his life. (The moms in our group sewed together T-shirt quilts for their sons using athletic uniforms and other memorable attire they had saved.)

At these events, moms can share stories and siblings can add their comments, but most important are the father's words. At the high school ceremony, every father affirms every son, not just his own. After all, by that point in time, the dads have come to know the heart of each young man, and this kind of sharing is a powerful testimony to the kind of community and fellowship that father-son groups are all about.

Meeting Format

We set forth various expectations for people joining our father-son groups. The commitment that fathers and sons will faithfully attend the meetings is foundational. The willingness to actively participate by expressing themselves verbally should be clearly understood (we want every boy and every man to share at least one comment and express at least one prayer out loud at each meeting, however brief). And respect for one another in our greetings is exhibited by a firm handshake and making eye contact when greeting each other.

As the time comes to begin meeting together, it is important to organize each father-son fellowship time in a way that will be successful. We define success in terms of enjoyable and meaningful interaction, learning something new about spiritual growth from God's word and real life experiences (refer to www.fathersons.org and Appendix B of this book for curriculum ideas), involvement in group prayers, and a commitment that "what is said here stays here."

To help pave the way for these things to occur, take a look at this set-up:

1. Begin the session with at least thirty minutes of **fun** time. Let the sons play outside (if possible) as the dads discuss the evening's topic. This is an important time for building relationships, and it should be a priority at each meeting.

2. After you call the boys in, ask them a **warm-up question**. Sometimes you may want to follow up with the same or a similar warm-up question for the dads. Avoid questions that have only one answer—and have some answers in mind to

help generate discussion. The kind of question that works well is "What choices or decisions between right and wrong have you had to make this past week?"

3. Present the **information and facts** that comprise the heart of your message. Include specific Bible verses.

4. Ask **questions to both gauge and increase understanding.** These will also facilitate a discussion of what the information means to the men and boys. You could, for example, ask, "How can we tell the difference between right and wrong?" and "Why is it so difficult to choose what is right?"

5. Conclude by **summarizing** your information and the biblical truths you've shared. Emphasize one or maybe a few key points that you wish to highlight.

6. Ask **application questions** to encourage the boys to make practical, everyday life changes based on the message they just heard. Here's an example: "Now let's take a moment for each son to discuss with his dad (or sponsoring dad) who you will be with this weekend. Will those people encourage you to make good choices? Which friends should you make a priority to spend time with?"

7. **Pray out loud** together. Do your best to encourage every father and every son to pray, even if they pray only a few words.

8. The meeting should end with **dessert** or some other fun activity.

Leadership Recruitment and Scheduling of Activities

Establishing a new father-son group can occur as early as 1st grade, but we have generally focused on 6th grade as an important time to get new groups formed. With this in mind, the work to establish a new group is typically been initiated with a network of the fathers of 5th grade boys.

Key to starting a strong father-son group is the determination of a group leader and a leadership team. These dads will ideally commit for multiple years of service, if possible. At the first leadership meeting, decide who will be invited to participate in the group (just church people? members of other churches?). Then set a start-up date for the initial "dads only" meeting for all potential participants. Also assign individual leadership responsibilities: let different dads be responsible for communication, the regular social events, service projects, etc.

Appendix B of this book provides a possible schedule of meeting topics for groups starting in 6th grade and continuing through high school. Meeting occasionally just for fun is an important part of the overall schedule. Social events are an important part of the toolkit for building relationships between fathers and sons, between fathers and boys who are not their sons, and between the boys themselves. These fun activities—scheduled for every third or fourth meeting—also add variety to the calendar.

Father-son groups have enjoyed bowling, laser tag, volleyball, dodge ball, go-cart racing, paintball, indoor rock climbing, and hikes.

Other special events include year-end family potluck dinners, picnics with games, campfires (on the beach, at the lake, in the mountains), coed parties with games and music, Christmas parties with singing and storytelling, talent shows at home or at church, and weekend retreats.

Working together on a service project at least once a year has also been an important part of the father-son experience. Groups can help clean up church facilities, do maintenance or minor construction projects for nearby ministries, prepare and distribute food at a local rescue mission, and help plant or harvest vegetables for a local food bank.

Father-son meetings also benefit from guest speakers and the use of video resources. Groups that stay together through the years will develop their own style as they respond to circumstances and as the leaders are directed by God. There will also be challenges along the way. Be flexible and creative and persistent. Each challenge will also bring opportunities for fathers and sons to grow together.

Sons get to experience first hand how godly men can reconcile their differences in a respectful and healthy manner, speaking the truth in love. Similarly, the boys must learn to look beyond external differences and discover the joy of both extending and receiving the unconditional love available in Christian fellowship.

Learning to be Inclusive

Christians do not always achieve an appropriate balance between inclusiveness and close-knit fellowship, and then our fellowship with one another may be too easily regarded as a closed circle or clique. Christian students in particular can become so focused on one another that their fellowship is a poor example to others on campus. So we dads attempted to teach our sons that our father-son fellowship group should not exclude those who want or need to be a part of it.

We kept our father-son network open for anyone to join; the only requirement was the desire to keep the boys focused on friendships with boys in the same grade. But even so, we made exceptions and welcomed four young men who were a year ahead in school because no other father-son group existed at that grade level.

One result of this open-door policy was that our sons were better equipped to be aware of fellowship needs in others. Case in point: some of the sons in our group had noticed that a young man on their high school campus (whose family attended our church) did not seem to be actively involved with other Christian guys.

During the process of reaching out in sincere friendship, the young man became actively involved in our father-son group, hanging out with us during teaching times and fun times, and participating in coed parties hosted at our homes. As a result of reaching out in this way, my son gained a lifelong friend, and I grew very close to our new FAST group member and his dad as well. Evidence of this bond is found in a note written inside my son's high school yearbook by the young man discussed above:

**Words cannot describe
what your friendship has meant to me.
You are such a special individual,
with a beautiful heart for the Lord.
Thanks for being such an inspirational person in my life.
I will forever cherish our friendship.
We have shared some unbelievable memories together,
and I hope our friendship will never end.**

These are not typical high-school yearbook sentiments between guys, but God had worked in powerful ways to build a brotherhood amongst the young men in our father-son group. It is real life example of how "iron sharpens iron," of how men can inspire one another to be better men, and how genuine friendship can be the result. And, by God's grace, with the group's focus on inclusiveness, lives were changed for the better and for eternity.

Successful male leadership of these groups can benefit from something special: a vital level of support and encouragement from women (wives and mothers). Of course, men must remain dedicated to the entire process of meeting together with their sons. But the appropriate involvement of moms in the decision-making process is helpful to the formation of father-son groups. Their encouragement and prioritization of FAST meetings in the family schedule can help keep things moving in a positive direction. Women will sometimes also organize themselves to pray regularly for the group's leaders, the meetings, and the relationships that will be developed between the men and boys.

From a Woman's Perspective
By Jan Kraushaar

FAST didn't happen fast. The ideas were percolating in the minds of several people for years. On a broad scale, they have been implemented in different ways for centuries, based on Deuteronomy 6 and other similar scriptures.

While the dads were working hard at their careers, meeting together in men's bible studies, and praying and hoping to be the best husbands they could be, their wives were developing friendships with each other and were praying together for godly relationships for their sons and daughters and husbands. Through the years we grew close to each other's children and their families as we taught Sunday school classes, chatted in driveways for carpools, coached or watched our children's sporting events, and attended church activities.

During the elementary years, our boys were becoming friends with each other at Sunday school and church camps, along with attending school and playing sports together. However, since some of them attended different elementary campuses or were home-schooled, we knew that it would be challenging to maintain those friendships as they moved on to different middle schools and high schools. As we parents watched our boys approach adolescence, we wanted them to solidify their Christian friendships and also to reach out to others and form new relationships. We knew that godly friendships in the teen years would be vital to our boys' spiritual health and growth. We women hoped that our husbands would continue to mentor their own sons, and that other men in our church would influence our sons as well.

The idea to form a new father-son ministry was born from this network of like-minded people – men and women coming together to brainstorm, dream and share their hopes for their children and the vision God was revealing to them. Fathers And Sons Together™ was developed, and a few years later, a similar group for mothers and daughters was formed.

God knit together our FAST fellowship during summer evenings at neighborhood pools, and barbecues at parks, and gatherings at pizza parlors, frozen yogurt stores and homes. At some of these homes, women taught the boys cooking skills as well as social skills.

Our sons learned how to be polite young men and warm conversationalists. Our group shared amazing meals together – homemade tamales, beef tacos, grilled hamburgers, baked beans, salads, yummy brownies and ice cream sundaes.

The women watched and prayed and baked cookies in the kitchen as fathers and sons gathered to ask hard questions, explore a range of topics, and learn together from God's word. Each father had a turn at leading the Bible study, but John was most instrumental in making sure that our FAST group continued throughout the years until the boys graduated from high school.

There are so many wonderful memories. We women smiled as the men did all sorts of things together, such as building bird houses, serving meals at shelters, helping at church clean-up days, jumping off cliffs into the ocean, and launching water balloons. Through the years women wrote countless e-mails and made phone calls to remind men of upcoming meetings. We helped organize special events and honored our young men with hand-stitched memory quilts for their high school graduation.

We had some hard times, but God was the center of those times as the source of hope and strength. There were health crises, difficult decisions, economic trials, and other struggles, but our men and boys were able to confidentially discuss these things together and support each other. FAST helped our sons develop into men and also strengthened our husbands. Glory to God!

Even though FAST was a group for men and their sons, we mothers had a vital role in supporting and praying for our men, helping them behind the scenes whenever we could. And our FAST group was a thriving fellowship for seven years, allowing our sons and their fathers to become friends for life.

Just as Mothers Of Pre-Schoolers (MOPS) and Moms-in-Touch were ministry inspirations for women, FAST has been my favorite ministry concept for the men in our Christian community. And just as MOPS and Moms-in-Touch have grown and still thrive today, I'm hoping that FAST will impact many communities and grow in the years ahead.

Appendix B

Overview of Meeting Topics
6th Grade through 9th Grade

The goal of the *Fathers And Sons Together*™ (FAST) ministry is to establish fellowship groups that provide an opportunity for fathers and other male mentors to nurture and guide the spiritual growth of their sons. The ministry has been successful at all age groups, from 1st grade to 12th grade. The following schedule is provided as an aid in the organization of lessons from this book and from the FAST website for 6th grade groups and older. Lesson plans and "biblical portraits" are available at **www.fathersons.org**. The publication "How to Start a FAST Ministry or a Grade-Level FAST Group in Your Church" is also available at **www.fathersons.org**.

SIXTH GRADE

Summer before 6th grade or early fall

Dads Only Meeting #1
Present highlights from chapters 1 and 6 of this book ("Relationships Define the Real Man," "Don't Embrace the Generation Gap", "Breaking from the 'Drop Off' Culture"), introduce the five main principles for becoming a real man (Appendix C), and ask for volunteers to fill leadership roles.

Father Son Retreat
At some point during your day or weekend together, dads should discuss the meeting format (Appendix A of this book) and establish leadership roles for recreation, fellowship, teaching, and prayer.

Fall through spring of 6th grade
Father-Son Fellowship Meetings

> **Dads Only Meeting #2**
> Finalize the year's schedule (this is always a challenging task – meeting times have varied between mid-week evenings, Friday evenings, and Sunday afternoons; occurring every other week, every third week, or once a month).

1. Welcome - Leader(s) explain purpose (to discuss important spiritual things together, and to have fun as well). Teach/discuss "Real Men Don't Just Go Along with the World - A New Mindset" (FAST website, lesson 1A)

2. Expectations - Reinforce goal of spiritual growth and give an overview of the five principles of spiritual maturity for men (Appendix B). Teach/discuss "Real Men Don't Just Go Along with the World - A New Network" (FAST website, lesson 1B)

3. FUN! (Bowling, laser tag, dodge ball…)

4. "Noah: One Man Who Made a Difference" (FAST website, biblical portrait)

5. "Real Men Don't Just Go Along with the World - A New Purity" (FAST website, lesson 1C)

6. FUN! (Bowling, laser tag, dodge ball…)

7. "Real Men Don't Just Go Along with the World - A New Honesty" (FAST website, lesson 1E)

8. "A Real Man Does What God Wants - Knowing God" (FAST website, lesson 2A)

9. FUN! (Bowling, laser tag, dodge ball…)

6th grade Meetings (continued)

10. "Jesus: Religion NO, Relationship YES" (FAST website, biblical portrait)

11. "Real Men Do What God Wants – A Dynamic Connection" (FAST website, lesson 2C)

12. FUN! (Bowling, laser tag, dodge ball…)

13. "A Real Man Does What God Wants - Trusting God" (FAST website, lesson 2B)

14. "Abraham: Chosen and Tested" (FAST website, biblical portrait)

Dads Only Meeting #3
Schedule the upcoming advancement ceremony, get the dads thinking about a "father's blessing" for each son (Appendix A), and encourage them to help each son discover a "life verse"

15. "Hide It in Your Heart" - Sons memorize the five-part definition of godly manhood and their life verse. Discuss/walk through the advancement ceremony

16. FUN! (Bowling, laser tag, dodge ball…)

17. "It's a Brave New World!" - Discuss the world of middle school. Invite a responsible eighth-grader and his dad to talk about the transition

18. "Martha and Mary: Two Sisters Who Prioritized a Loving Relationship with God" (FAST website, biblical portrait)

19. 6th Grade Advancement Ceremony (perhaps dinner with families). Sons recite the five principles of maturity and their life verses. Fathers bless their sons.

SEVENTH GRADE

Summer before 7th grade or early fall

> **Dads Only Meeting**
> Review key points from chapter 7 of this book ("Let's Get Real"). Emphasize importance of openness and trust in upcoming talks that will include personal male issues. As Eric Wolf has stated, "It is not what is said in a small group that will kill it, it is what is not said. Groups have to be as safe as possible for the men and the boys." Ask for volunteers to fill any open leadership roles, and discuss the schedule/format of meetings.

Fall through spring of 7th grade
Father-Son Fellowship Meetings

> 1. Review key points which were addressed during the 6th grade meetings regarding "A New Mindset" (website lesson 1A), "A New Network" (website lesson 1B), "A New Purity" (website lesson 1C), "A New Honesty" (website lesson 1E), "Noah" and "Martha & Mary" (website biblical portraits)

> 2. Review key points which were addressed during the 6th grade meetings regarding "Knowing God" (website lesson 2A), "Trusting God" (website lesson 2B), "A Dynamic Connection" (website lesson 2C), "Abraham" and "Jesus" (website biblical portraits)

> 3. FUN! (Bowling, laser tag, volleyball, dodge ball…)

> 4. "Real Men Don't Just Go Along with the World – Sexual Boundaries" (FAST website, lesson 1D)

7*th* grade *Meetings* (continued)

5. "Joseph: Purity, Integrity, and Perseverance" (FAST website, biblical portrait)

6. FUN! (Bowling, laser tag, volleyball, dodge ball...)

7. "A Real Man Leads with a Servant's Heart - Accepting Responsibility at Home" (FAST website, lesson 3A)

8. "Isaac and Jacob: The Woes of a Passive Father and a Passive Son" (FAST website, biblical portrait)

9. FUN! (Bowling, laser tag, volleyball, dodge ball...)

10. "Daniel and His Companions: Tested by Fire" (FAST website, biblical portrait)

11. "A Real Man Leads with a Servant's Heart – Kindness and Sincere Love" (FAST website, lesson 3E)

12. Service Project (work at a nearby ministry, soup kitchen; help single moms or elderly with home/lawn maintenance, etc.)

13. "A Real Man Leads with a Servant's Heart – Earning Money" (FAST website, lesson 3B)

14. "Solomon: A Man of Great Wisdom – And Great Foolishness" (FAST website, biblical portrait)

15. FUN! (Bowling, laser tag, volleyball, dodge ball...)

16. "A Real Man Builds Relationships - Making Friends" (FAST website, lesson 4A)

17. "Barnabas: Encourager and Relationship Builder" (FAST website, biblical portrait)

7*th* grade Meetings (continued)

> **Dads Only Meeting**
> Schedule and program the year end sports day, and discuss possible summer activities.

> 18. "Real Men Don't Just Go Along with the World – A New Integrity" (FAST website, lesson 1F)

> 19. Year-End Picnic: Softball game and potluck dinner with FAST families

EIGHTH GRADE

Summer before 8*th* grade or early fall

> **Weekend Adventure or Service Project**
> Camping, backpacking, river rafting, surfing, fishing, hunting, or equestrian, and/or major service project (church or other ministry building repairs, camp maintenance, etc.)

> **Dads Only Meeting**
> Discuss sex/dating issues and attempt to reach a consensus or at least an understanding about how these topics will be addressed. Ask for volunteers to fill any open leadership roles, and discuss the schedule/format of meetings.

Fall through spring of 8*th* grade
Father-Son Fellowship Meetings

> 1. Review key points which were addressed during the 7th grade meetings regarding "Sexual Boundaries" (website lesson 1D), "A New Integrity" (website lesson 1F), "Kindness and Sincere Love" (website lesson 3E), "Making Friends" (website, lesson 4A).

8th *grade Meetings* (continued)

2. "Real Men Don't Just Go Along with the World – A New View of Women" (FAST website, lesson 1G)

3. "Paul: A Daring and Earnest Love for People" (FAST Website, biblical portrait)

4. FUN! (Bowling, rock-wall climbing, volleyball, go-cart racing...)

5. "A Real Man Builds Relationships - Corporate Prayer" (FAST website, lesson 4C)

6. "Nehemiah: Vision and Leadership Guided by Prayer" (FAST website, biblical portrait)

7. FUN! (Bowling, rock-wall climbing, volleyball, go-cart racing...)

8. "Real Men Look Beyond This Life – A New Destiny" (FAST website, lesson 5A)

9. "Bethel: A Vision, A Place, and a Personal Connection" (FAST website, biblical portrait)

10. FUN! (Bowling, rock-wall climbing, volleyball, go-cart racing...)

11. "A Real Man Looks Beyond This Life - Perseverance" (FAST website, lesson 5B)

12. "David: From Success to Failure, From Guilt to Freedom" (FAST website, biblical portrait)

13. Service Project (work at a nearby ministry, soup kitchen; help widows or seniors with home/lawn maintenance,etc.)

8th grade Meetings (continued)

14: "A Real Man Looks Beyond This Life - Courage and Joy" (FAST website, lesson 5C)

15. "A Real Man Builds Relationships – Friendships for Life" (FAST website, lesson 4B)

16. "Rahab: An Example of Life-Changing Choices" (FAST website, biblical portrait)

17. Transition to High School (discuss expectations)

18. YEAR-END FUN! (Bowling, rock wall climbing, volleyball, go-cart racing...)

NINTH GRADE

Summer before 9th grade or early fall

Dads Only Meeting
Determine a meeting schedule that fits with high-school activities and demands (Sunday afternoons often work well), discuss the staging of coed activities/parties and views regarding music, dancing, etc. during high school, and ask for volunteers to fill any open leadership roles

Fall through spring of 9th grade
Father-Son Fellowship Meetings

1. Review key points which were addressed during the 8th grade meetings regarding "A New View of Women" (website lesson 1G), "Corporate Prayer" (website lesson 4C), "A New Destiny" (website lesson 5A), "Perseverance" (website lesson 5B), "Courage and Joy" (website lesson 5C)

9th *grade Meetings* (continued)

2. "Real Men Don't Just Go Along with the World – A New Respect for Women" (FAST website, lesson 1H)

3. "Real Men Do What God Wants – A New Way of Life" (FAST website, lesson 2D)

4. FUN! (go-cart racing, paintball, rock climbing…)

5. "A Real Man Leads with a Servant's Heart – Spending Money" (FAST website, lesson 3C)

6. "A Real Man Leads with a Servant's Heart – Saving Money" (FAST website, lesson 3D)

7. "A Real Man Leads with a Servant's Heart – Marriage for Life" (FAST website, lesson 3E)

8. FUN! (go-cart racing, paintball, rock climbing…)

9. "A Real Man Builds Relationships – What Real Women Want" (FAST website, lesson 4D)

10. "A Real Man Looks Beyond This Life – Difficult Questions, Part 1" (FAST website, lesson 5D)

11. "A Real Man Looks Beyond This Life – Difficult Questions, Part 2" (FAST website, lesson 5E)

12. Service Project (work at a nearby ministry, soup kitchen; help widows or seniors with home/lawn maintenance, etc.)

13. "A Real Man Looks Beyond This Life: Difficult Questions, Part 3" (FAST website, lesson 5F)

14. "A Real Man Builds Relationships – Outreach, Sharing Our Faith" (FAST website, lesson 4E)

9*th* *grade Meetings* (continued)

> 15. "A Real Man Does What God Wants - Loving God" (FAST website, lesson 2E)

> 16. Year-End Social Event: Potluck dessert with FAST friends and families

TENTH GRADE—TWELFTH GRADE

Continue discussing key topics, with an emphasis on moving from the fundamentals of faith in Christ to an active daily relationship with Him that changes us and matures us. Find fresh approaches to the five-part definition of a godly man.

Incorporate practical sessions on how we are to live, and focus on the issues we face as men:

- Traffic Safety/Accident Prevention
- Diet and Health
- Pornography
- Internet and Cell Phone Use
- Drug and Alcohol Abuse
- Sports and Competition
- Politics and Justice

And the list does go on. Know your son, and you'll know the issues to address.

End with a high-school graduation ceremony that includes an opportunity for men who have now gotten to know each son to express perceptions of their passage into the world of men—specifically, into the world of *godly* men.

Appendix C

Summary of Spiritual Maturity Principles for Men

The following list is a good framework for teaching about real life godliness because it is derived from the many truths for faithful living that we find throughout Scripture. The five main principles also enable a simplified yet meaningful discussion of the question "What are the characteristics of a mature Christian man?"

May these principles motivate our sons (and us dads as well) to turn to God's Word for guidance and to find in the Lord courage in the face of conflict, wisdom in the face of difficult decisions, and hope in the face of life's difficult times.

1. A real man does not go along with the world.

1a. Real men think differently about life's choices than many of the people around them, because they have been changed within. Real men are careful about whom their friends are, and they have the strength of character to say no to wrong activities and bad people.

1b. Real men set boundaries for their thoughts and behaviors. They don't automatically go along with what the world says is OK, and they thoughtfully evaluate their level of participation in its attractions. Real men work together to keep one another strong, and they develop strategies for helping one another resist, reject, and, when necessary, recover from harmful behaviors.

1c. Real men don't lie and cheat to get ahead in the short-term. They are more interested in character development, spiritual growth, and the Lord's long-term rewards than they are in dishonest gains that won't last.

1d. Real men treat women with respect and value their noble character above any other aspect of beauty. During the dating process and throughout their life, relationships with women are characterized by kindness, honesty, and healthy boundaries.

2. A real man does what God wants him to do.

2a. A real man knows his heavenly father intimately and therefore trusts that our all-powerful, all-wise, and all-loving God has his best interests in mind. This trust encourages a real man to stay close to God.

2b. A real man continually listens for God's guiding voice so that he can be sure of doing what God wants. A real man's identity, sense of direction, understanding of right and wrong, and actions all stem from a mind influenced by the Holy Spirit.

2c. Real men acknowledge God as supreme in their life. They find joy in celebrating Him with other believers because He alone is worthy of their complete love and respect.

3. A real man leads with a servant's heart.

3a. A real man understands and embraces his roles as faithful husband and loving father. With God's help and in His divine power, a real man responds to the biblical call to serve as a spiritual guide in the home. When disciplining his children, he combines unconditional love and sound instruction with training and correction.

3b. As wise stewards of God's resources, godly men are responsible with money. They are both industrious and generous.

3c. Real men are kind to their spouse, parents, sons and daughters, friends and opponents, co-workers and clients, strangers and neighbors. They are sincerely respectful of the people around them.

3d. A godly man is passionately committed to his wife and willing to do whatever it takes to preserve the marriage and make it a place of joy and fulfillment.

4. A real man builds relationships.

4a. A real man is not a loner: he works at being a good friend, he cares about other people, and he knows he needs to maintain meaningful relationships with believers.

4b. A real man prays with other believers. He is confident about God's listening ear, yet he approaches the Lord's throne in humility. He gets to the point in expressing his thoughts, and he is attentive to what the Lord may express to him through the Holy Spirit.

4c. A real man takes an active interest in the people around him, regardless of their religion, culture, or worldview. He invites them to have fellowship with God just as he does, but he is also attentive to their level of interest. He does not know how they will respond, so he rests in the power and movement of the Spirit and only speaks of what he knows.

5. A real man looks beyond this life.

5a. Real men look beyond what they encounter in this world. Their life is colored by a rich understanding of their destiny with Christ, a secure future that is anything but dull. Despite the corruption brought into this world and into our human nature by sin, godly men see glimpses of that divine future glory in worshipful music, the joy of loving relationships, moments of restful contentment, the beauty of nature, teamwork and healthy competition, great literature and fine arts.

5b. Real men don't give up when the journey is rough. They keep a long range perspective through the bad times as well as the good times. Choosing to keep a biblical view of God firmly in their mind, godly men don't lose heart.

5c. Real men don't give in to fear, and they do not let themselves be overcome by worry. They face tough decisions with courage, and they find joy in life despite difficult circumstances because they know God cares for them, is with them, and is at work in the situation.

5d. God leaves us with many tough and unanswered questions—and a real man is OK with that. He does not shy away from intellectual discussions about his faith, he humbly acknowledges what he does not know, he prayerfully pursues answers to tough questions as he studies the scriptures, and he shares the truth (as he best understands it) in love.

Appendix D

Difficult Questions

Have you noticed that our Christian faith does not give easy answers to some of the significant questions that the difficulties of life raise? One reason is that our faith is not some neatly unified man-made theory. It offers us a glimpse of God: it shows only what he has chosen to reveal and what he deems vital for us to know.

The most important components of spiritual knowledge that God has chosen to reveal are fairly basic, such that people are able to understand: He loves us, He has provided a way for us to know and love Him, and living in relationship with Him is the only way to live. That message of who He is and who we are to be and how we are to live is life-changing, exciting, and beautiful, and it calls for a personal response from every person who hears it. An appropriate response on our part includes the acknowledgement that God is God and I am not.

While we certainly don't know everything about our God and His ways and we don't have answers to all the questions prompted by life in this fallen world, we who call ourselves Christians are aware of the power and presence of Jesus Christ in all that is known to us. He is not a bystander.

He is the image of the invisible God,
the firstborn over all creation.
For by him all things were created:
things in heaven and on earth, visible and invisible,
whether thrones or powers or rulers or authorities;
all things were created by him and for him.
He is before all things,
and in him all things hold together.
— Colossians 1:15-17

Difficult questions arise as we consider the truth that God is actively involved in this world. For example, will we accept that God's power is unlimited and His character is all loving even when bad things happen to those we love?

Our sons will ask the same tough questions that we wrestle with. We all want to be able to understand and explain to others the truths about God. But this quest is difficult because God is who He is, and He is certainly not obliged to answer all of our questions based upon our schedule. One of the truths we discover along the way is that our questions, our sorrows, our frustrations, and our issues must take a back seat to His agenda and His purposes.

Will we surrender to His authority and accept His timeline? Can we draw close enough to Him as our spiritual father and older brother to accept and even appreciate who He is, despite our limited understanding of what is going on in our world? Will we trust in His love for us in the middle of hard times, despite society's ridicule, and, in some places in this world, at risk of our life?

Question #1: Why Do Good People Suffer?

Let's address one of many difficult questions we Christians wrestle with: If our loving Father, perfect Friend, and infinitely wise Counselor loves us and watches over us, why does He allow people to suffer?

Each of us can easily identify many different sources of pain and suffering, including some that we recognize as appropriate, such as punishments for crimes, the consequences of foolish decisions, and the intentional pain involved in physical training. What we struggle with most, however, is "senseless" suffering or those times when good people are unjustly victimized by evil or a natural disaster.

In my view, one compelling answer to the basic question of why God allows suffering is our **freedom,** being able to act and live as we choose without being subject to another's control over our decisions and actions. God created us in His image: like Him, we are volitional and capable of exercising our will. Unlike Him, however, our decisions are constrained to the options available in this world, and our actions are subject to natural laws applicable to this world.

Genuine freedom—even when it is limited as ours is—brings with it real consequences. Specifically, if we were not able to make our own decisions and thereby choose between pleasure and pain—and if others were not able to make their own decisions and choose between pleasure and pain—then none of us would actually have free choice. God created a world, however, in which we do have freedom to choose, and real consequences result from our decisions.

With our freedom comes the possibility that we will choose evil, and the outcome is pain and suffering, often impacting "good" or "innocent" people. God could eliminate that kind of pain and suffering by taking away our freedom of choice, by removing all negative outcomes of our choices, and thereby forcing us to make only good decisions. With that removal of our free will, however, we would not be the unique persons that God desires to have a relationship with. God could also remove every disruptive act of nature (floods, fires, storms, earthquakes), but the more we learn about ecosystems, the more we appreciate the cumulative and positive impact such events have on the overall balance of nature.

The personal pain we experience—for whatever reason—invites us to consider the bigger picture: God can use the pain we experience in this life to remind us that something is terribly wrong with this world and to prompt us to look more carefully at what life is all about. Is life limited only to what we experience in these bodies on this earth? If the truth is a resounding no—and if we have in fact been created with an eternal spiritual dimension—then we can view differently the temporary suffering we experience on this earth and hope for overwhelmingly positive spiritual outcomes from it.

We may also need to consider that our appreciation of pleasure (the feeling of happiness, delight, or satisfaction) is at least partly dependent upon our experience of pain and suffering. Familiarity with sadness enables us to appreciate joy, just as the experience of pain enables us to appreciate the absence of it.

Finally, in moments of spiritual insight, we are able to recognize that God uses pain to refine our character, to enable us to comfort others who are suffering, and to amplify our understanding of the eternal security we have in Christ.

> Praise be to the God and Father
> of our Lord Jesus Christ,
> the Father of compassion
> and the God of all comfort,
> **who comforts us in all our troubles,**
> **so that we can comfort those in any trouble**
> with the comfort we ourselves have received from God.
> — 2 Corinthians 1:3-4

Question #2: How Can We Understand Predestination?

The discussion of suffering and our free will raises another question: How do we reconcile man's ability to make good or bad choices with the apparent fact that God controls everything and even knows ahead of time what we will choose to do? In other words, how do God's will and our free will work at the same time?

This question raises the issue of time, a construct that enables us to distinguish events that occur at the same point in space by the interval between those events. We human beings think of time as a linear dimension where one moment follows another. For us, one moment disappears before the next one comes along.

For us, life consists of the past, the present, and the future. We can't change the past, we can only operate in the present, and our influence over the future is limited. We can't know with any certainty when another person or even we ourselves will make a life-changing decision that will impact the present as well as the future.

So, naturally assuming that God operates in time and space like we do, we struggle to understand the cosmic aspects of His power. After studying Scripture, however, many knowledgeable men and women have suggested that God is not constrained by time and space. Because He is the Designer and Creator of this world, we can reasonably assume that He is able to move in and out of these dimensions.

> Almost certainly God is not in Time.
> His life does not consist
> of moments following one another.
> If a million people are praying to Him
> at ten-thirty tonight,
> He need not listen to them all
> in that one little snippet we call ten-thirty.
> Ten-thirty—and every other moment
> from the beginning of the world—
> is always the Present for Him.
> — C. S. Lewis, *Mere Christianity*

Somehow it is possible for us to have freedom of choice in this life even though our Sovereign God Himself is involved in the unfolding of history, in global history as well as our personal history. We can't fully understand God's involvement, because he is not constrained by the dimension of time as we are.

> For a thousand years
> in your sight
> are like a day
> that has just gone by,
> or like a watch in the night.
> — Psalm 90:4

So there you have it. Our existence is governed by physical laws. Goodness and evil are part of all this because our freedom involves real choices and real consequences. Yet God is in control in ways that are well beyond these physical laws that govern us. Is He playing with us? Are His intentions good? Is He able to bring about what He wants for us? Can we trust Him?

In practical terms, when we attempt to reject the laws of nature or fail to recognize our ability to make right or wrong choices, reality hits us hard because things go wrong. When we act responsibly, things will still occasionally go wrong - it's part of the process of learning not to hold on to anyone or anything in this world too tightly. Jesus tells us to expect difficulty in this world, but He also reminds us who is ultimately in control.

> "I have told you these things,
> so that in me you may have peace.
> **In this world you will have trouble.**
> But take heart!
> I have overcome the world."
> — John 16:33

This world has a compelling attractiveness to us, and so we often assign great importance to our earthly experiences of happiness or sorrow. God invites us to broaden our view to include a life that is well beyond (and more significant than) the here and now. He informs us that our current reality is just a dot in the context of an eternity with Him. He is not playing with us. His intentions are good. He will bring about what He wants for us, and we can trust Him even though we do not understand the minor incidents or major problems that we encounter along the way.

> Trust in the LORD with all your heart
> and lean not on your own understanding;
> in all your ways submit to him,
> and he will make your paths straight.
> — Proverbs 3:5-6

A Small Sign

I awoke to a dimly lit room at the USC Norris Cancer Center, and Michael was thankfully snoozing. I shifted in the chair that had been my sleeping place periodically during the past 3 days, and nodded to my wife Jan who was also stirring in her chair. I reached across for her hand, and we prayed silently together, continuing our vigil. Our world had been changed with the discovery of our son's tumor a week prior. We both knew we would never be the same, but we didn't know much else at that point in time.

The small hospital room was occupied by Michael's bed, medical equipment, our two chairs, and some things delivered by friends and family. On the wall above Michael's headboard one of his friends had tacked a hand written sign on a piece of cardboard with a familiar bible verse - Jeremiah 29:11.

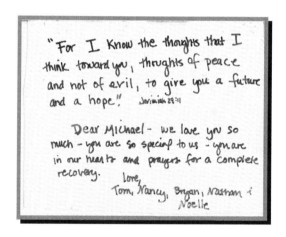

Jan and I both found ourselves pondering and discussing that verse during Michael's initial recovery stage. We thought we had grasped the meaning of it before, but waves of new understanding flowed over us as we emotionally released Michael to the hands of his heavenly father.

God knows the details of His thoughts and plans for Michael. We don't, nor does Michael. He has Michael's best interest at heart, not the self-centered perspectives that we lapse into. Michael will find peace and thrive under God's guidance and in His timing. He knows what is actually evil or harmful for Michael, not just what we perceive as being detrimental. He knows what is best for Michael.

He is the giver of hope. He provides for Michael's future. Jan and I only temporarily had a role as two stewards of a young man who belongs to God. Are we willing to accept God's plans, however different they are from our own?

A small cardboard sign taped to a hospital wall, given by a thoughtful friend. However it comes to us, the Word of God has a way of shaping us. It cuts to the center of an issue we need to address, opens our mind to life changing truth, reveals something important about what is happening in our midst, exposes us for what we really are, shines light on who He really is, and enables us to sincerely love Him and others.

In my own efforts to love family members and friends, I am continuously amazed at the complexity of each person. Just when I think I know how they will react or what they will choose, something they say or do takes me by surprise. That's the way of relationships. I am regularly humbled by my lack of understanding. Although I can't begin to understand what this God - whom I love and serve - will do from one moment to another, I have come to trust in His never failing love and goodness. I don't really get it, I can't explain it accurately, but He is my closest companion. Amazingly, He opens His arms to each one of us. Our heavenly Father embraces us as His adopted sons and daughters. Our spiritual big brother, the only begotten Son, wraps His arm around our shoulders. The indwelling Holy Spirit enables us to hear His voice. Then God shows us the way, one step at a time.

Additional resources for dads, including lesson plans and a how-to guide for setting up father-son fellowship groups, can be obtained at **www.fathersons.org**, a service of *Fathers And Sons Together*™ (a.k.a. FAST). FAST is a non-profit corporation located in Irvine, California, with associates based in Boulder, Colorado.

Acknowledgments

This book is about spiritual growth principles for fathers that I have learned from the Word of God and from other godly men and women. Some of these friends are now with the Lord. I think specifically of Wayne Anderson (encourager to my inner life as a believer and fellow admirer of the beauty of Laguna Beach), and Dick Wagner (friend and mentor early in my married life and survived by Ina Sule, namesake of our daughter).

For many years I have benefited from the teaching of Gary Stubblefield and other pastors including Craig Hill, Steve Olsen, Michael Risley, Ted Hamilton, Mike Sciarra, Chuck Corwin, and Dave Bennett. Their words of wisdom have clarified for me the biblical principles presented in this book, but they are certainly not responsible for any inaccuracies on my part in attempting to present the truth.

From the beginning of my commitment to follow Christ, the written works of beloved author C.S. Lewis have provided inspiration. Gratitude also goes to contemporary authors who have impacted my understanding of these issues, and motivated so many Christian men to grow up. To name just a few: Robert Lewis ("Raising a Modern Day Knight"), John Eldredge ("The Way of the Wild Heart"), James Dobson ("Bringing Up Boys"), David Bentall ("The Company You Keep"), Mark Holmen ("Faith Begins At Home"), and Stu Weber ("Locking Arms").

To my wife Jan, I still remember your return from the spring 1999 women's retreat. You were so excited to have found three kindred spirits (Heidi Joanou, Alisa Evans, and Jan Kraushaar) who wanted to connect our entering-sixth-grade boys. As an outcome of that initial effort to connect families, Michael and I were blessed with an awesome FAST band of brothers—and it's my privilege to have spent quality time with these young men and their dads: Matt Joanou, Jordan Evans, Kent Kraushaar, Chris Feicht, John Evancoe, Alex Pfotenhauer, Michael Bjorkman, Bryan Bedson, Jon Weissberg, Daniel Humphreys, Zach Cooper, and Andrew Fredericks.

To my son Michael, you have been tested by fire, yet you still maintain a steadfast closeness to your heavenly Father. I am impressed by your strength of character and I am also deeply touched by your faith, hope and love.

To my daughter Ina, you inherited many noble characteristics from your mother, but your unique giftedness (positive demeanor and athletic skills included) have added so much to our family life. You married a godly man, and together you and Joe are a blessing to many. These stories and parenting principles are yours to have and to share with future Cover generations.

To my father John F. Kain, your common sense and business acumen have been imprinted on each of your six children. You were a faithful husband to your soul mate Barbara, and I know you miss her deeply. Thank you for sharing your love of music with all of us. And to my father-in-law Nick Tankersley, you and Ruth have modeled an exceptional dedication to each other as well as your extended family. Your presence on the sidelines of many soccer fields and volleyball courts in earlier years, combined with recent participation in bible studies at our home with Yvonne and Sarah and Joyce, are small examples of "being there" for loved ones. Thank you for investing in things that really matter.

I want to thank Lisa Guest for her contributions as editor of the first versions of this book – she has upheld the FAST ministry in prayer for many years, while also supporting her husband Mike in his long-standing involvement in this ministry. I am also thankful for the advice and edits provided by Jan Kraushaar, and the word processing skills of Rachel Duff. The following men and women also offered constructive inputs and encouragement along the way: Tim Joens, Jim Burns, Joseph Parker, Jim Walton, Pete McKenzie, Steve Albin, Tom Lynch, Bill Fellers, Janet Andrews, Corrine Fredericks, Marlie Whiteman, Pam Cole, Ray Grijalva, Mark Vanlandingham, Richard Somerset, and the guys in my Wednesday morning bible study group and Thursday morning support group.

I wish to gratefully acknowledge Mark Humphreys for his leadership of FAST at our church and for partnering with me in the formation of FAST as a nonprofit organization. Finally, I am thankful to Eric Wolf who is spreading the message of FAST to Colorado and beyond.

The Author

John Kain is a dad who has been in the trenches with many other men who believe the next generation is worth fighting for. He is also a transportation planning consultant and volunteer leader of various Christian ministries in Southern California. He started Fathers And Sons Together™ (FAST) with several other dads in 1999. Since that time, John has prepared resource materials for FAST leaders and is currently encouraging the start-up of similar father-son networks at other churches.

President of Urban Crossroads, Inc., which he co-founded, John has been directly involved in the planning of sustainable transportation networks for many new towns in California and Colorado since the 1970's. He directs the firm's work on major planned communities and urban connectivity improvements.

John received a Master of Science degree in Administration from UC Irvine. He is a certified professional urban planner and a Fellow in the Institute of Transportation Engineers (ITE).

John and his wife Jan live in Irvine and Laguna Beach, CA. Their daughter Ina graduated from The George Washington University in 2006, and married Joe Cover in 2009. Their son Michael graduated from Vanguard University in 2010.

Made in the USA
Lexington, KY
26 May 2012